A Collection

Of Artwork

By

Maddy Chelmis

A BBTS Publication
Deri, Bargoed.
BBTS (Baarbaara The Sheep Publications)
Est. Feb 2012
email: **baarbaarathesheep@hotmail.co.uk**
baarbaarathesheep/wordpress.com

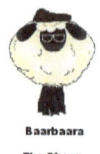

Baarbaara
The Sheep

© Maddy Chelmis - December 2023

ISBN-13: 9798870091860

Imprint: Independently published

KDP Assigned ISBN registered with Booksinprint.com

Original Artwork © Maddy Chelmis
Images by Mandy Tovey
Cover Design by Tog

Typeset Cambria

Dear Grampy, Merry Christmas and a Happy New Year!

I hope you know how much you mean to me. Your unwavering kindness never goes amiss. Your selflessness and support are appreciated much more than I can put into words here. There is no doubt that you are such a strong person, facing any challenges that come your way with decorum and determination. I am always amazed at your calm composure even during the most trying times, you inspire me to experience life to the fullest as you have proven that stress brings no value. There are many times when fond memories of times spent together appear in my head. Passing by the many pubs we enjoyed after school dinners in, reminiscing about strolls around the swan infested Cosmeston Lakes, even as far back as breaking my front tooth on the gigantic chocolate bar you got me in the flat! You have provided such safety and warmth to not only me, but my mum and Auntie Debbie, for that I cannot thank you enough. You are truly a very special man that has graced a lot of lives with your beautiful presence. I can only end by saying how much I love you, and how it is an absolute pleasure to call you my Grampy.

All my love, Maddy Xxx

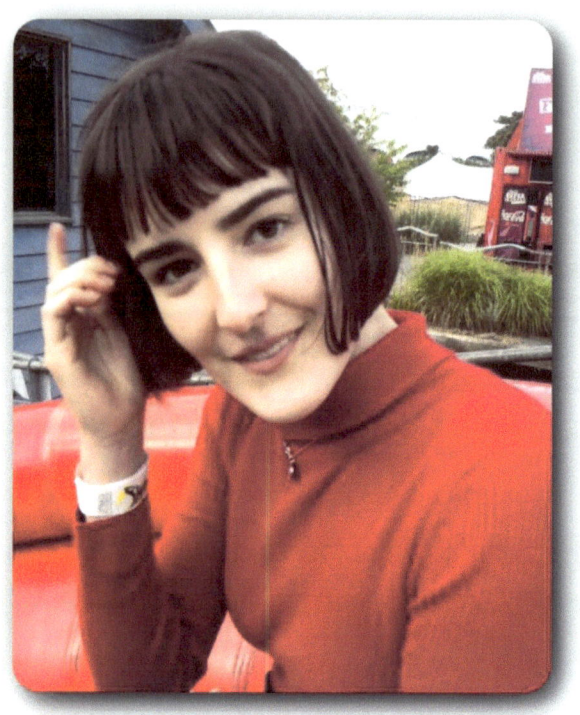

Biographical Notes:

Maddy Chelmis is a recent graduate from the University of Reading with a Bachelors degree in Art. Refining her practice with a focus on figurative paintings. Exploring themes of body acceptance and mental health, Maddy uses painting to express feelings and encourage emotional engagement with viewers.

Early Years

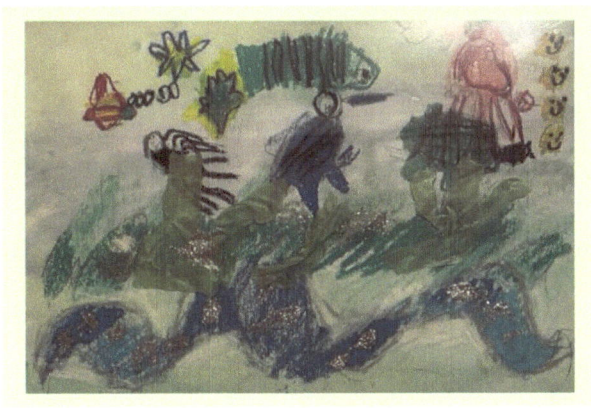

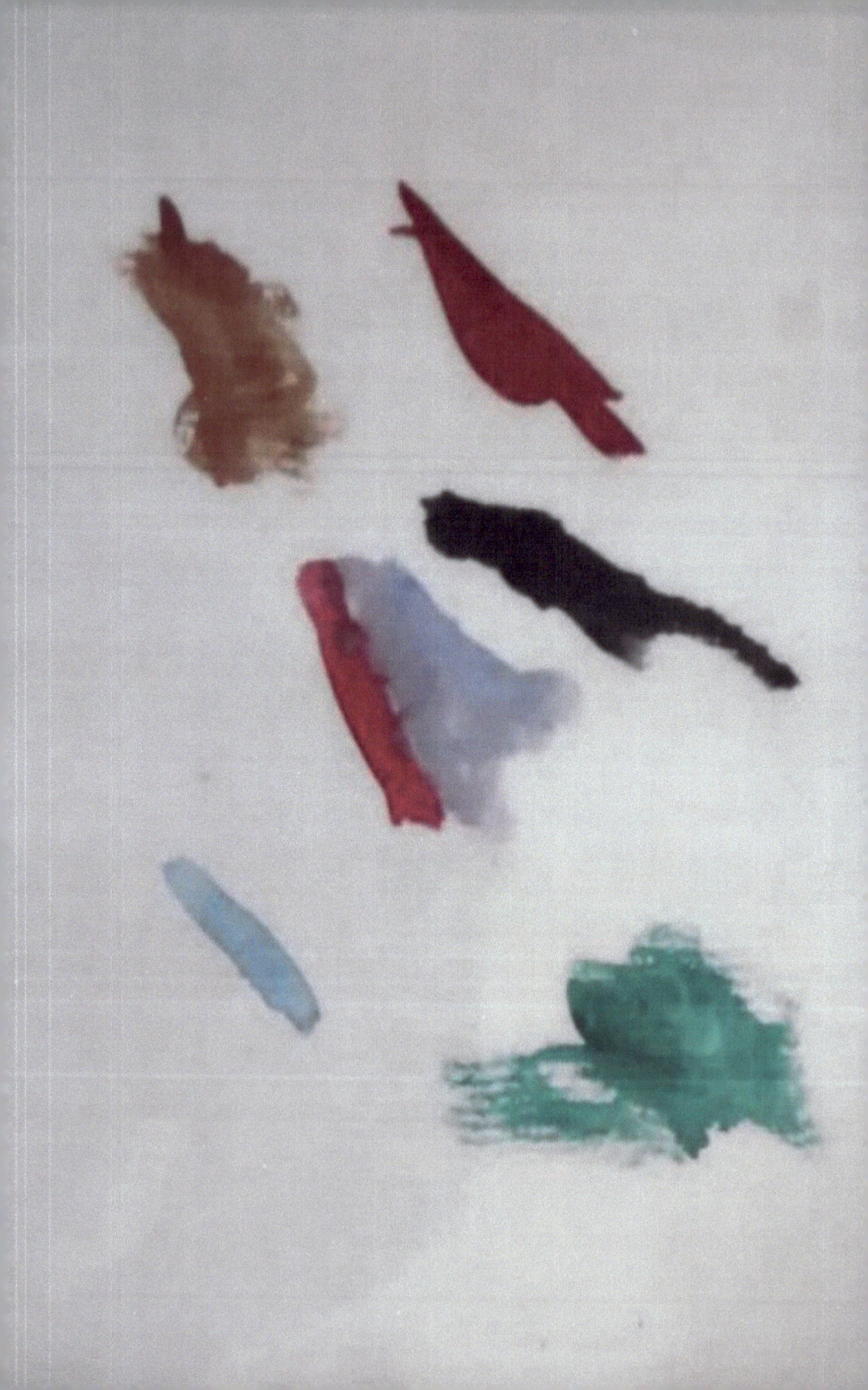

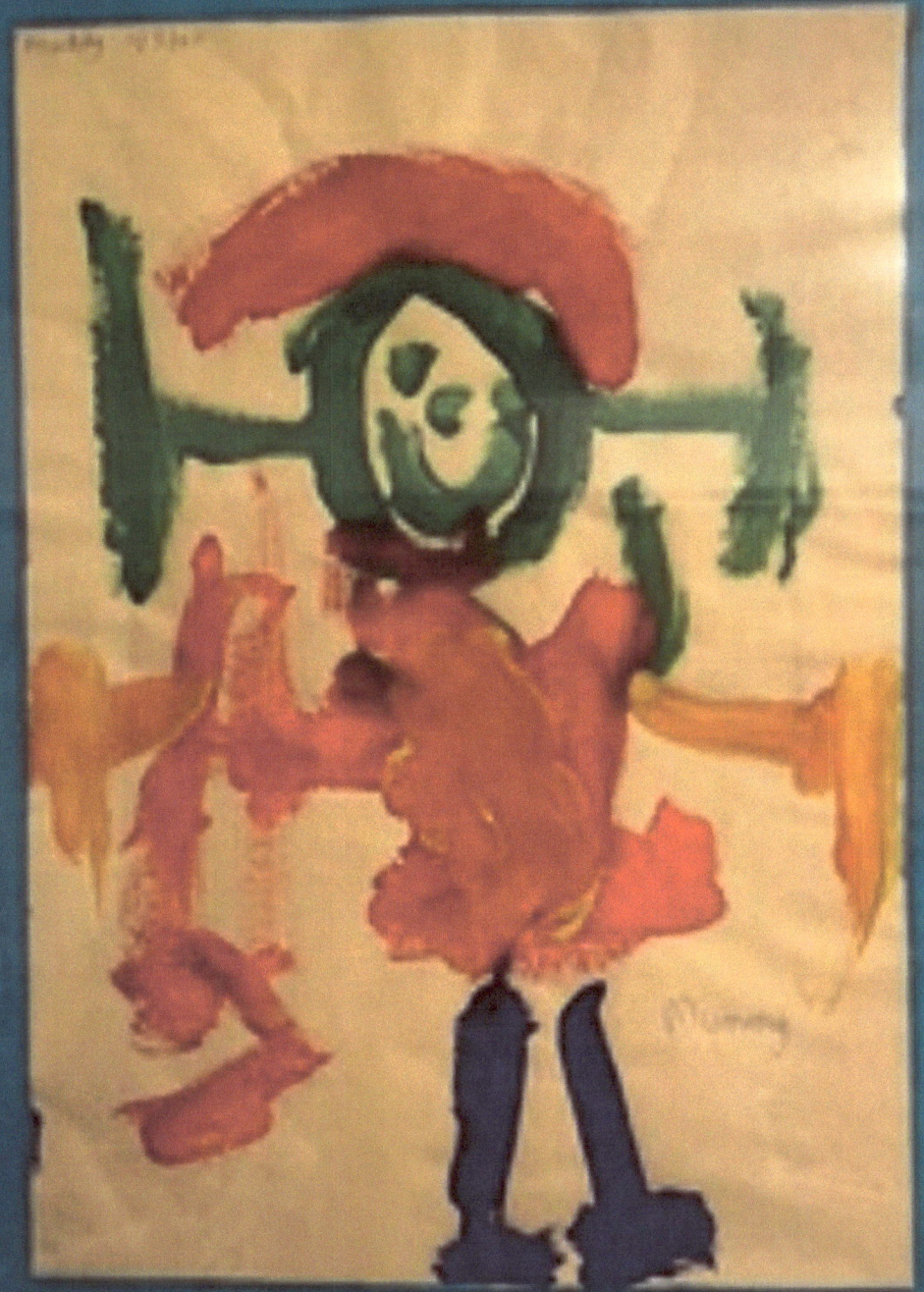

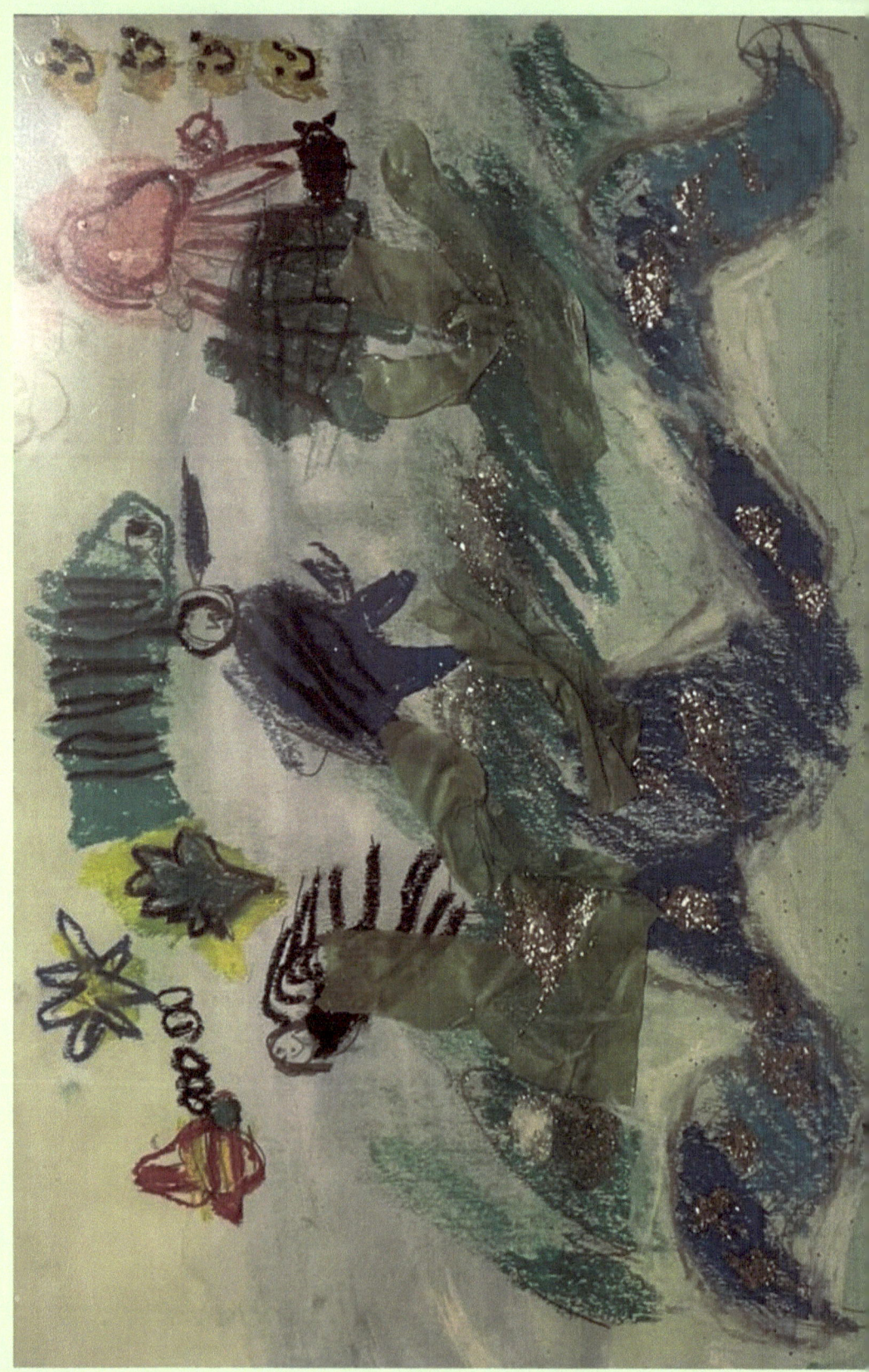

Portraits

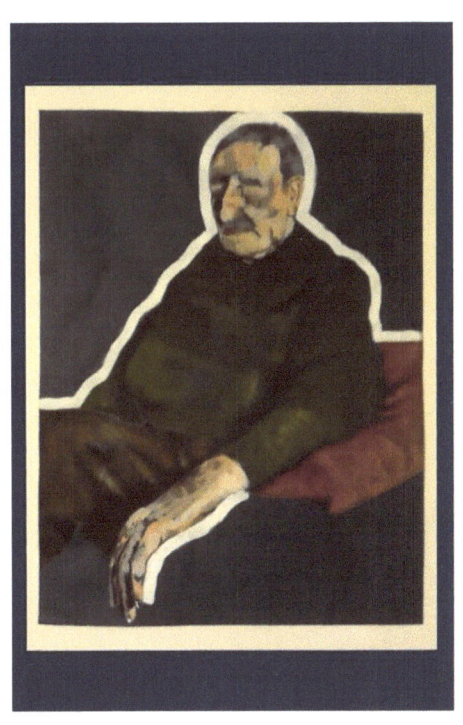

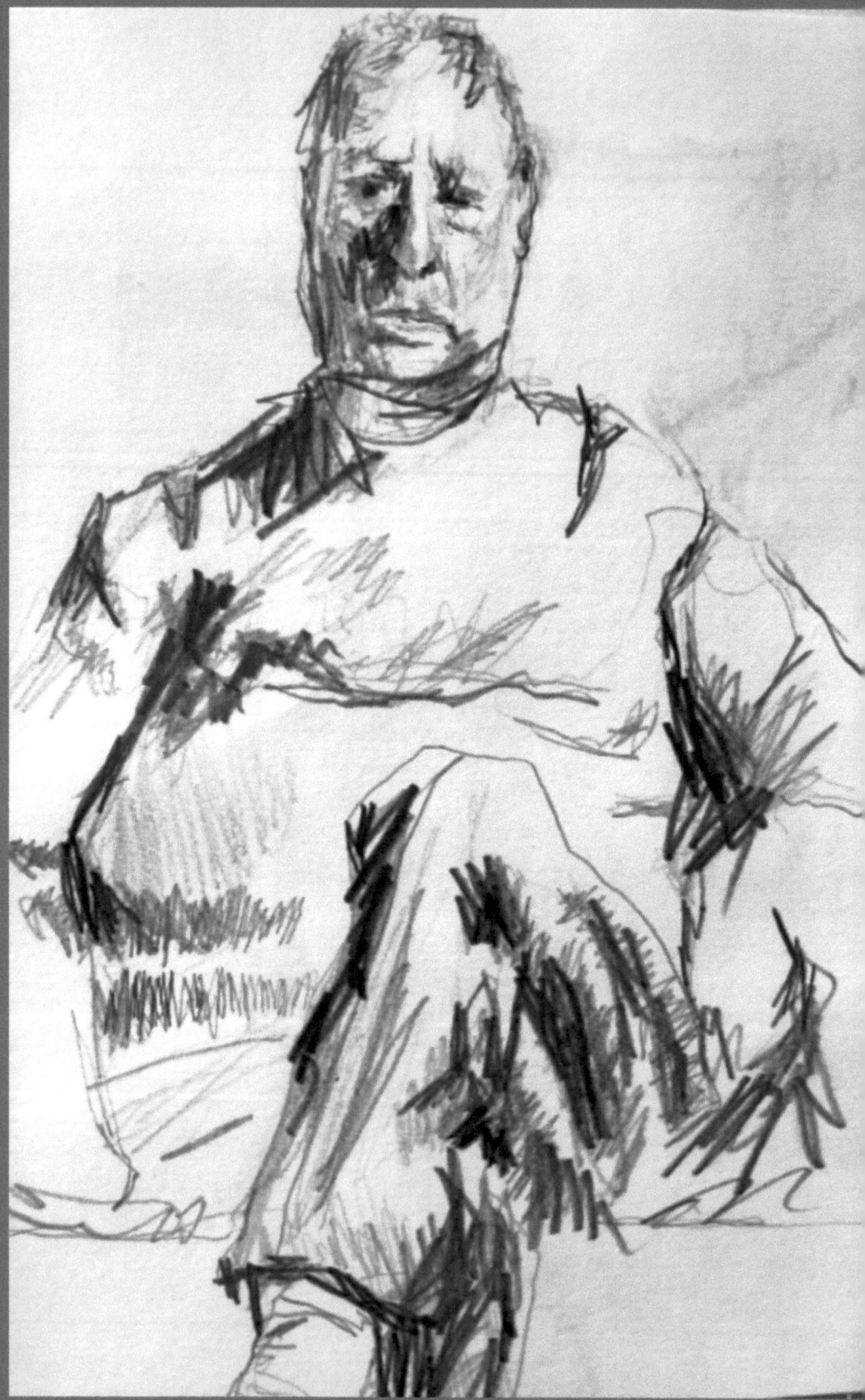

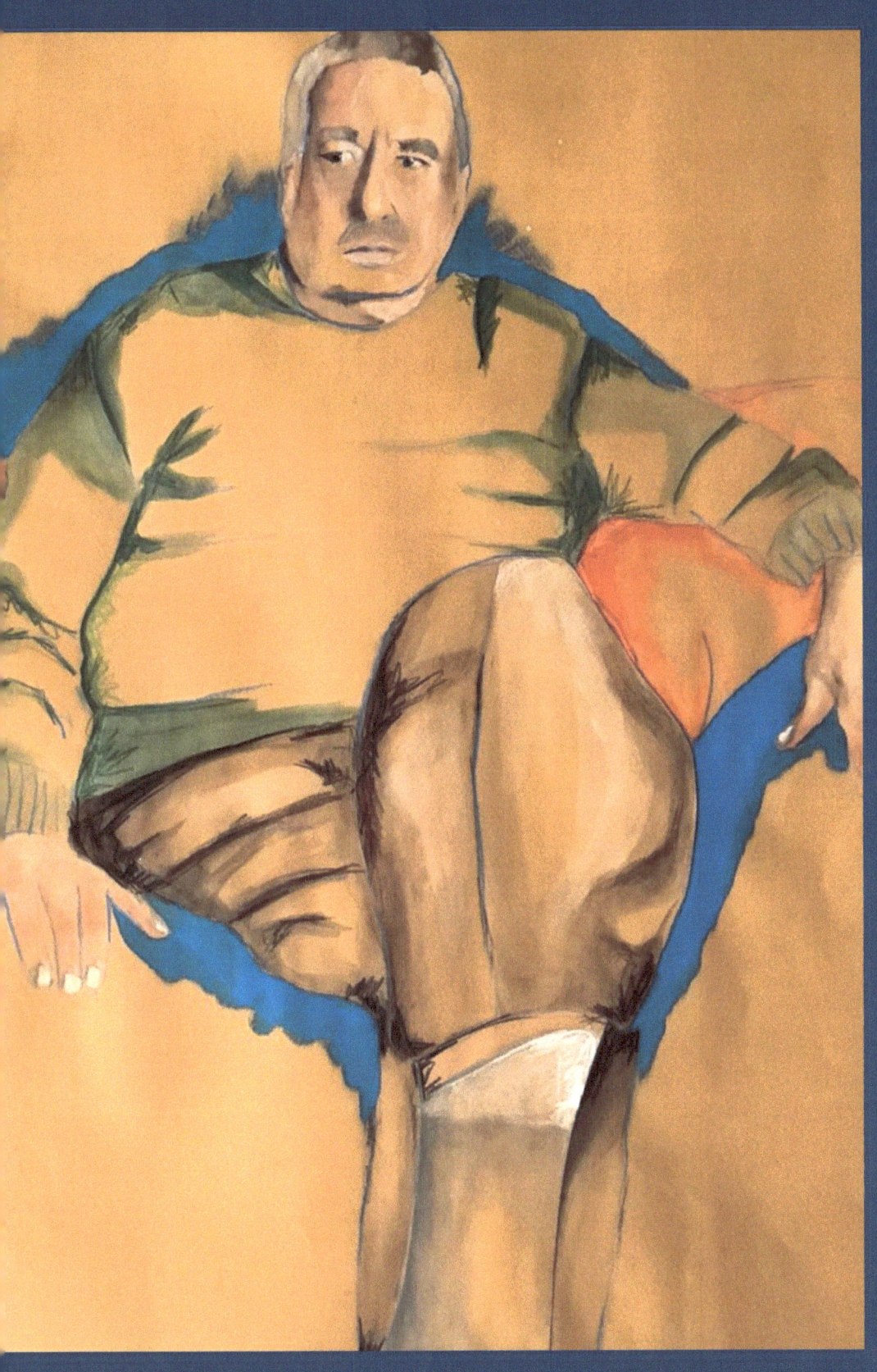

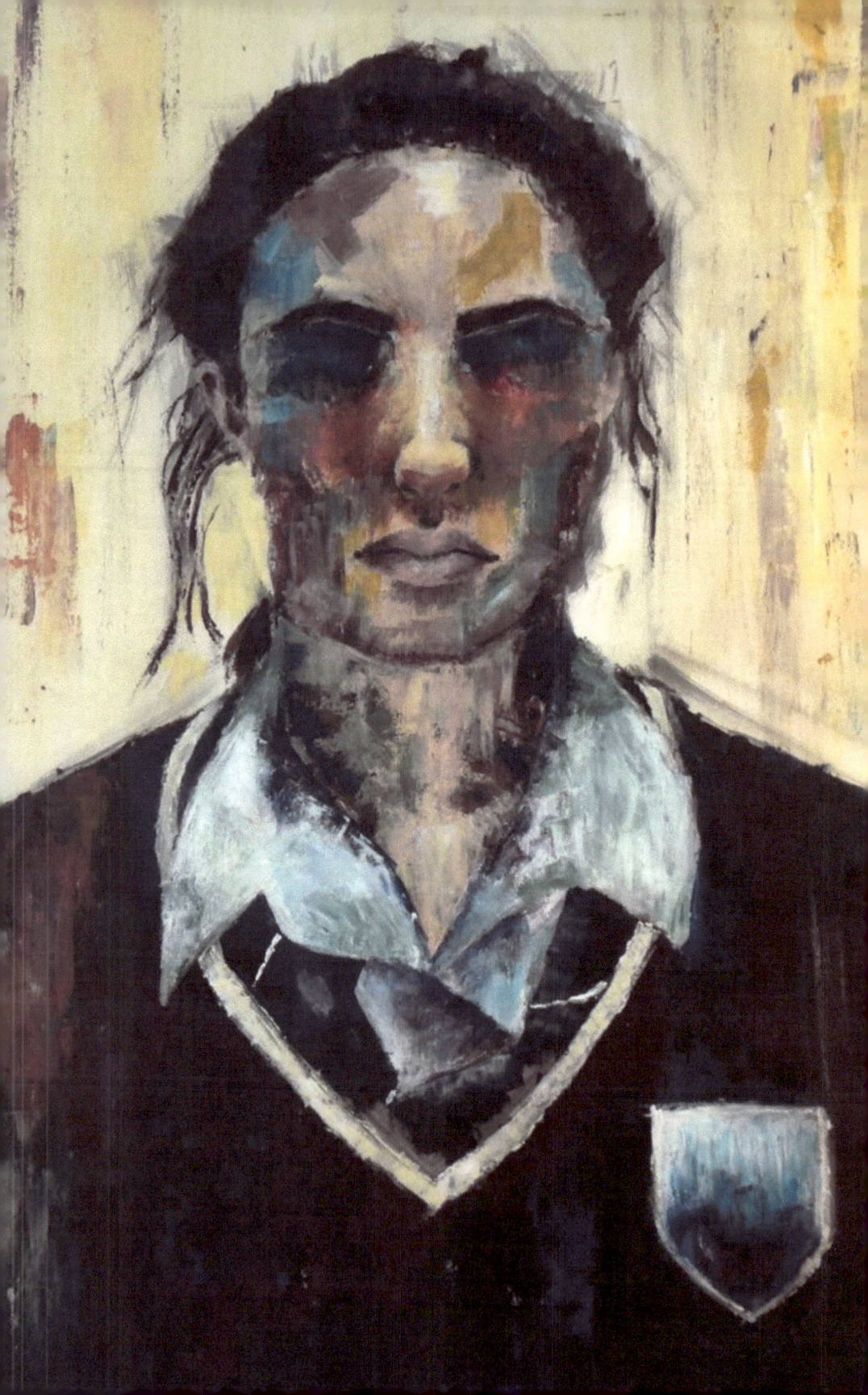

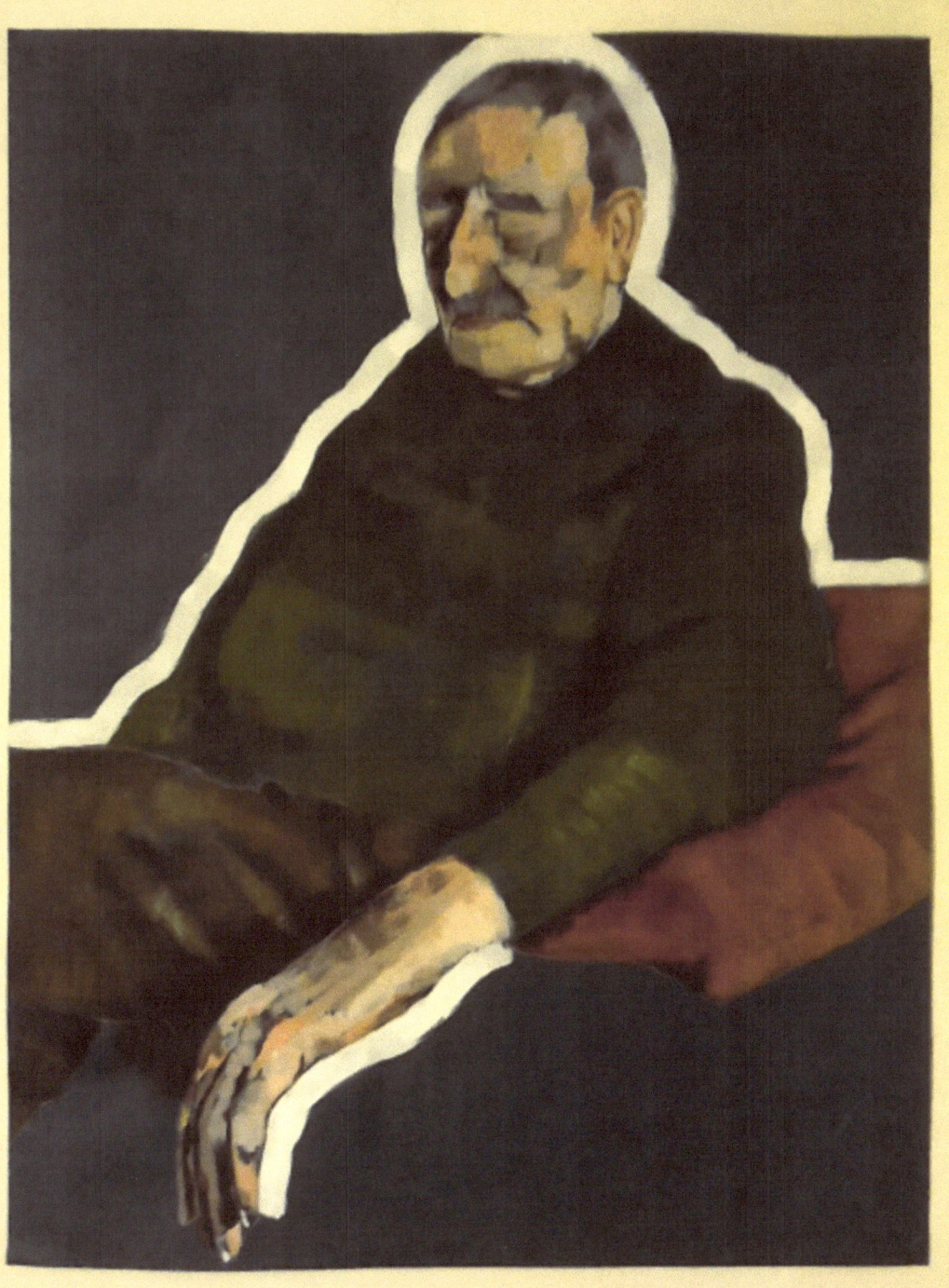

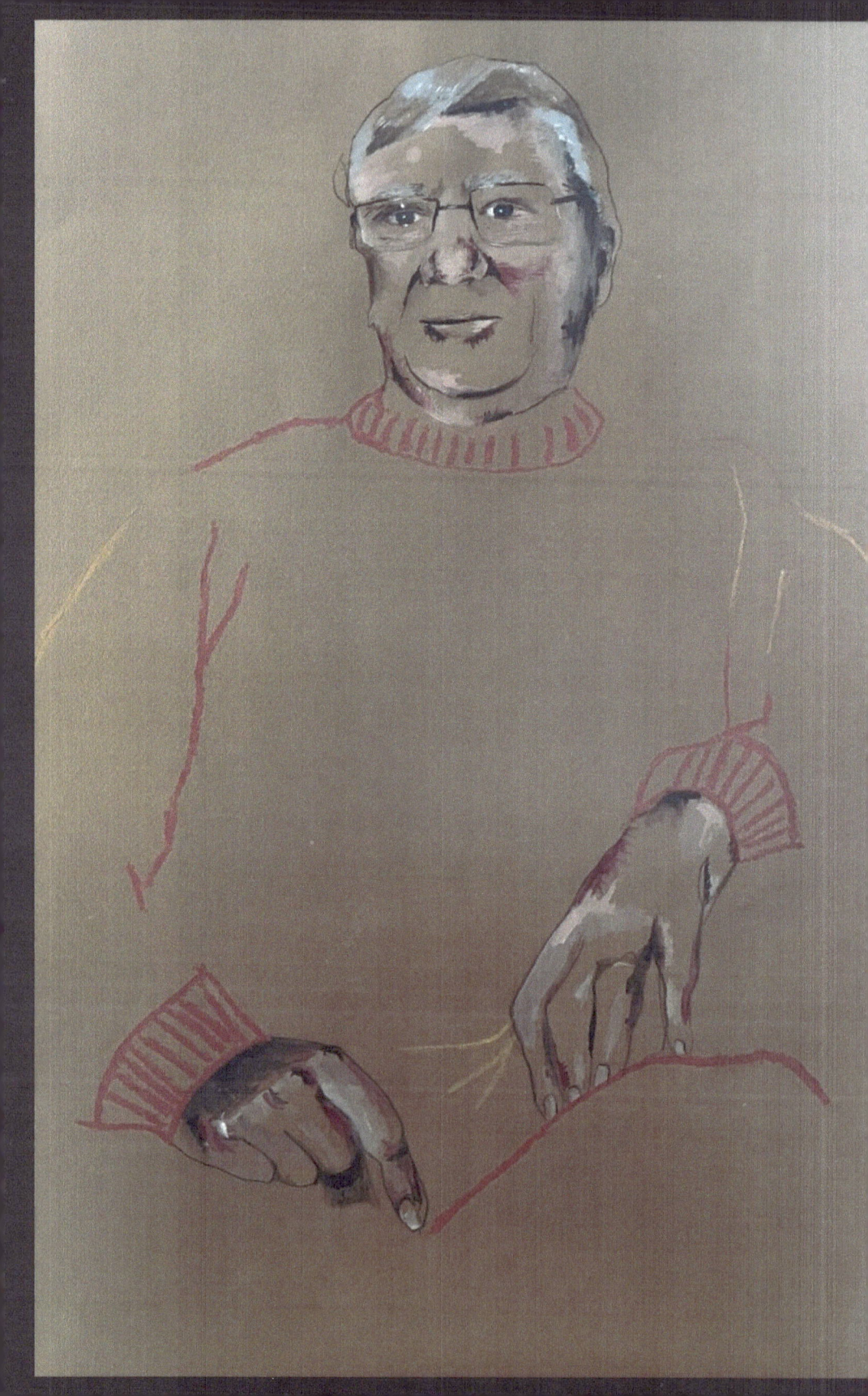

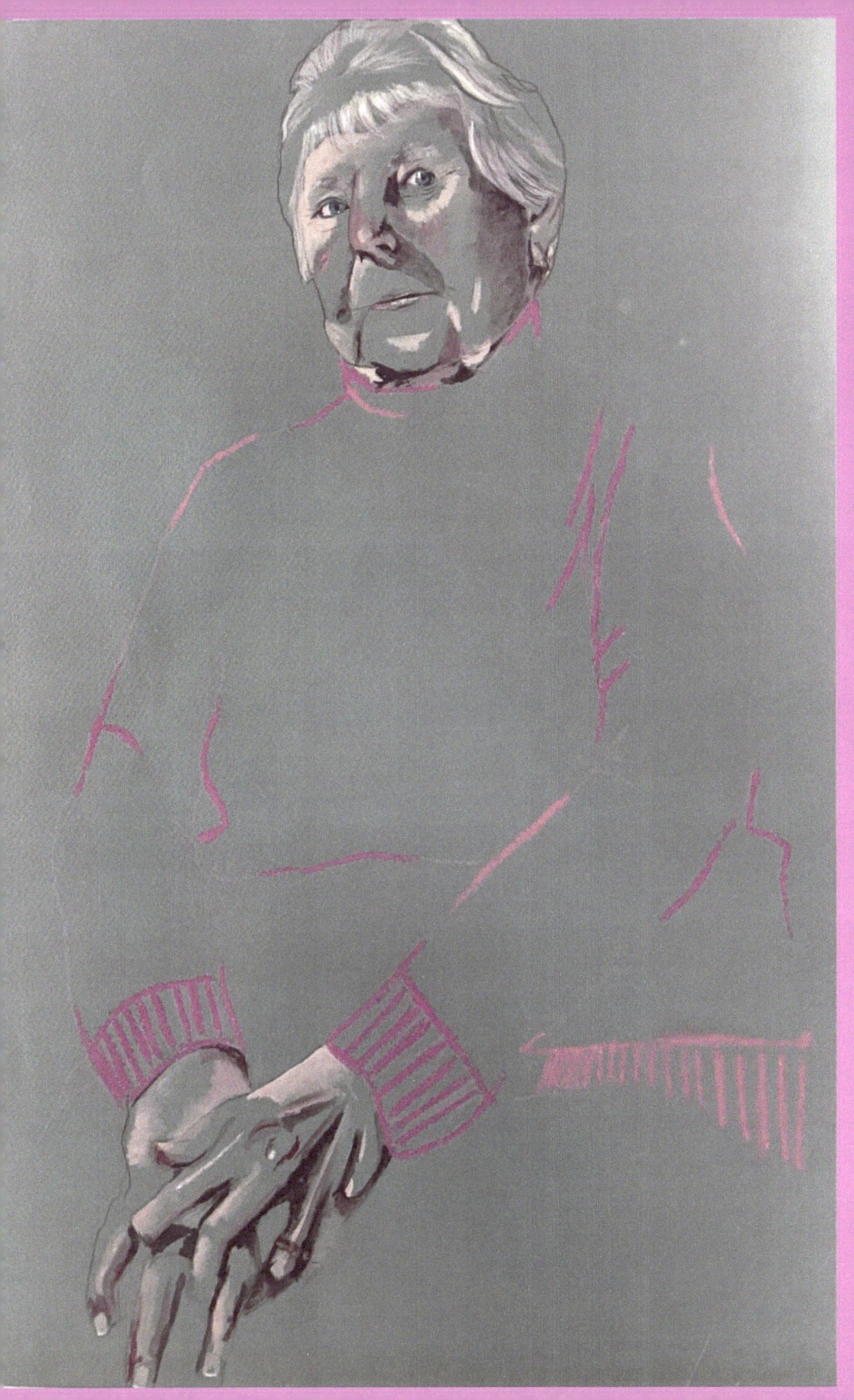

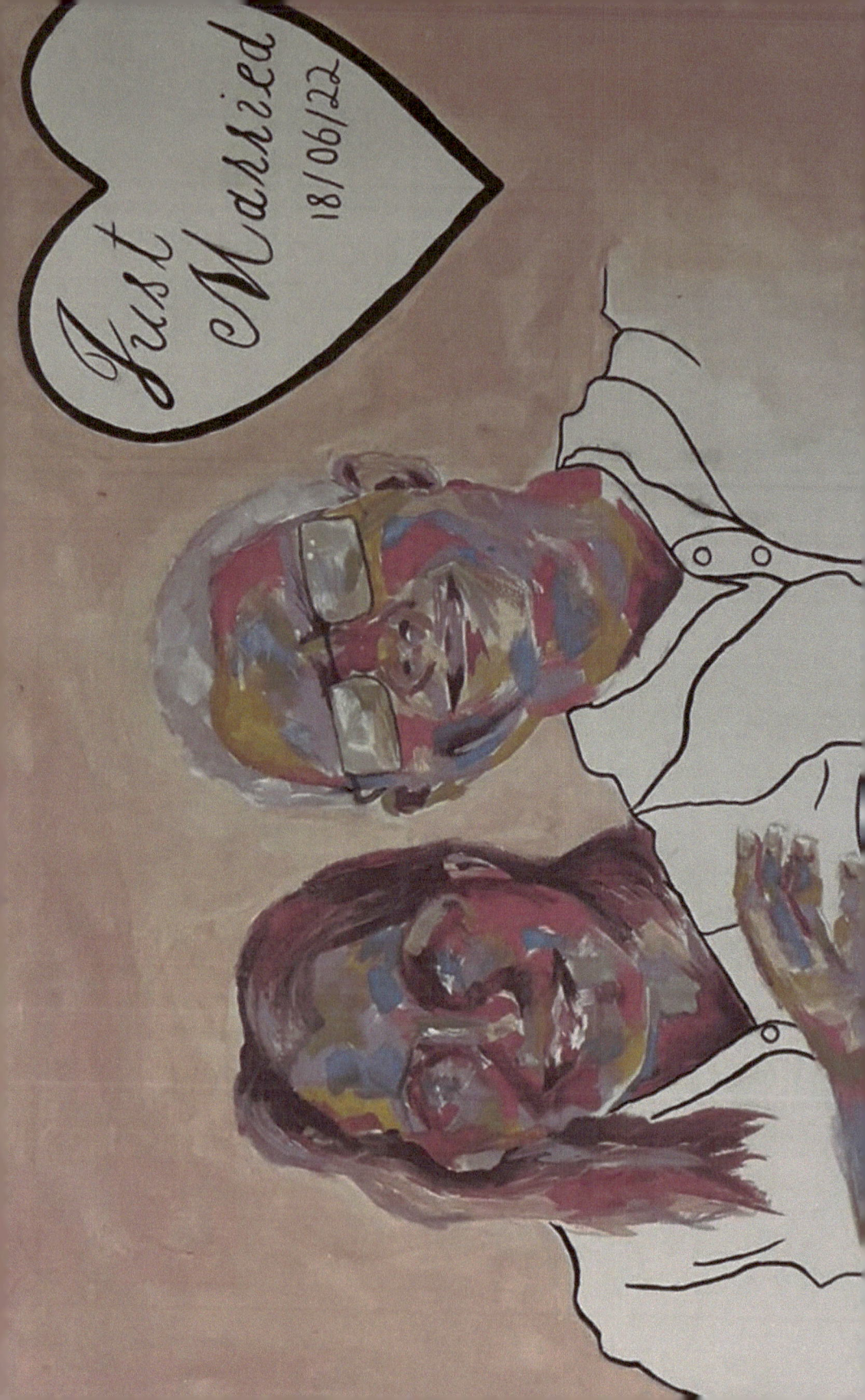

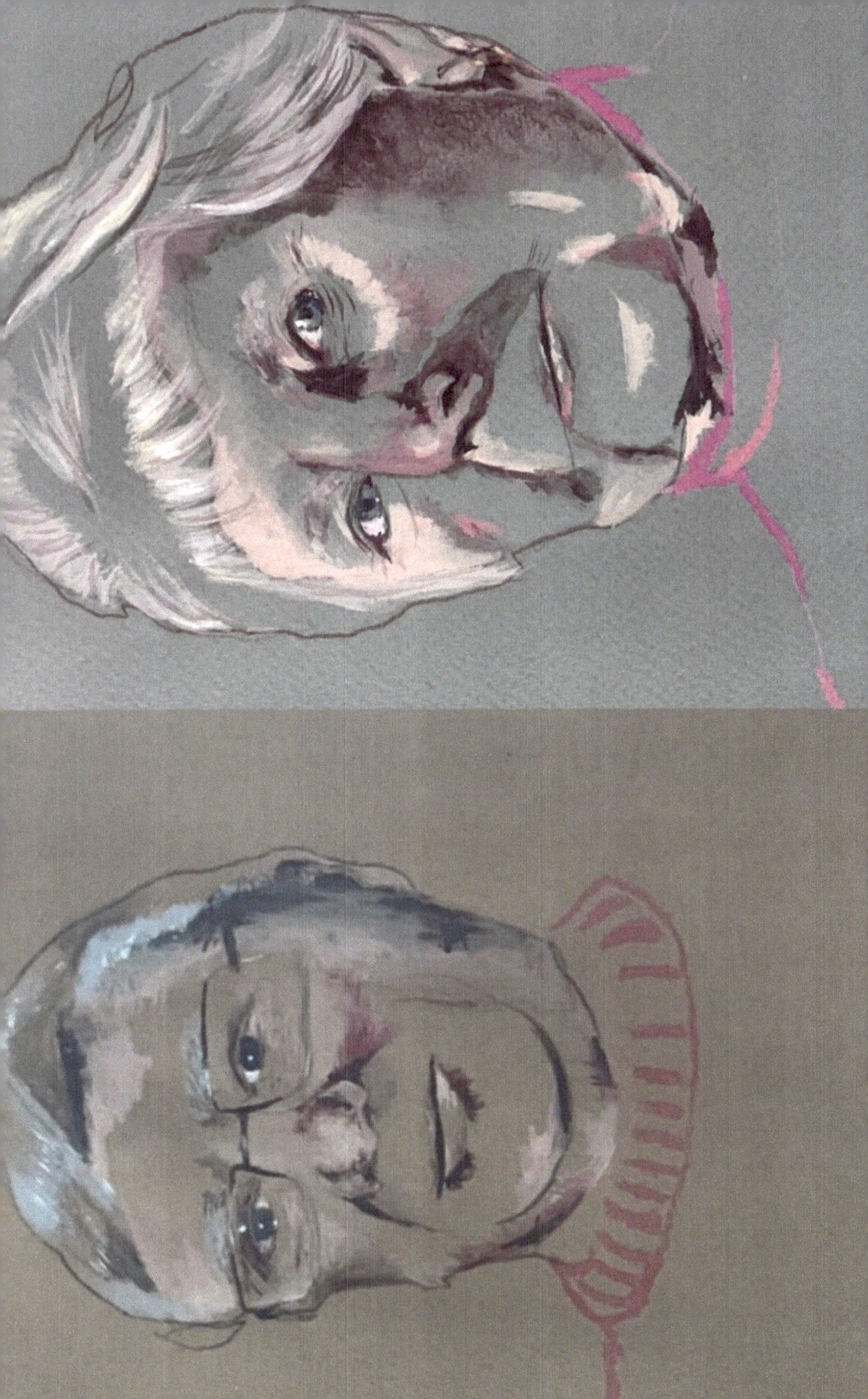

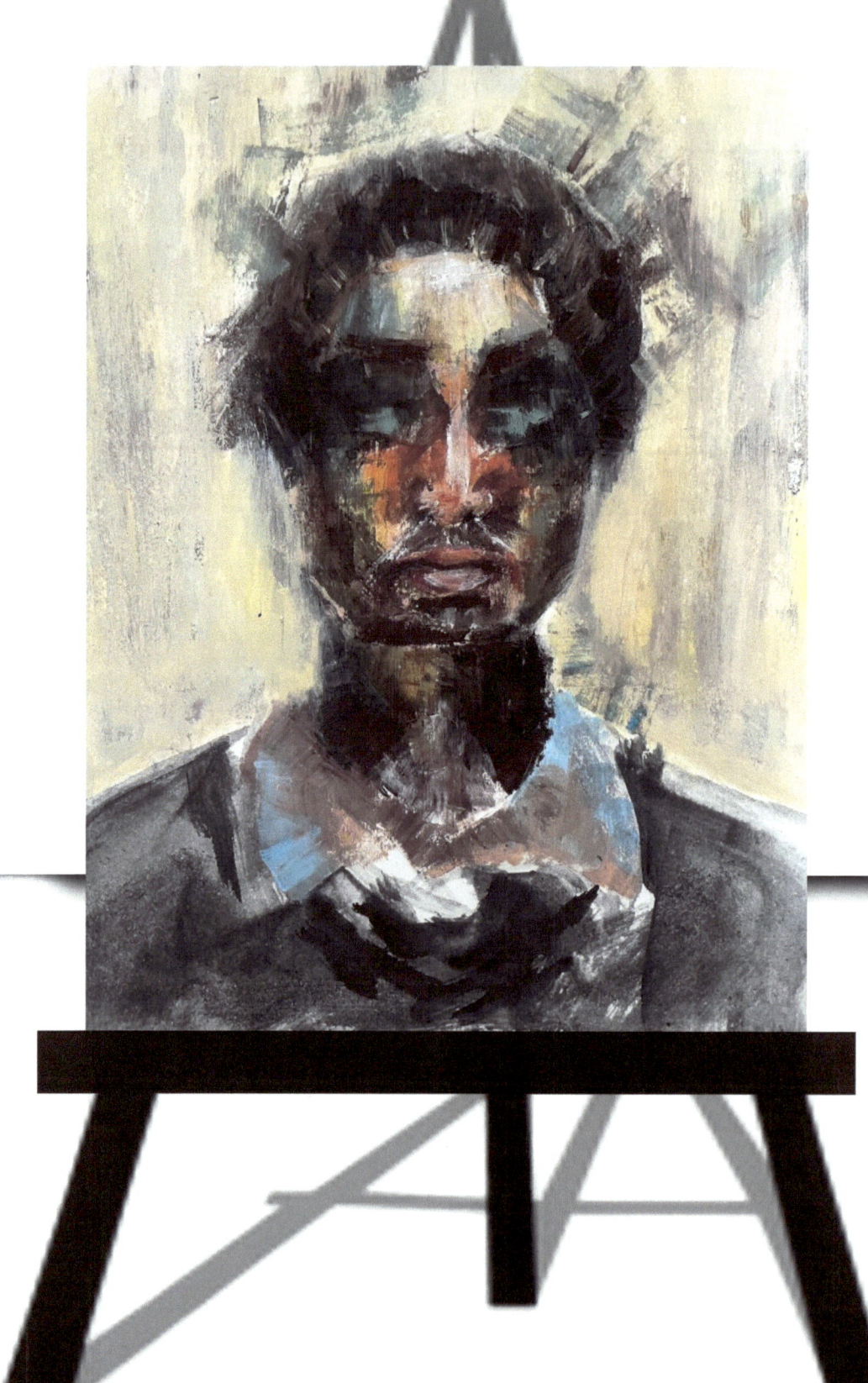

Abstract

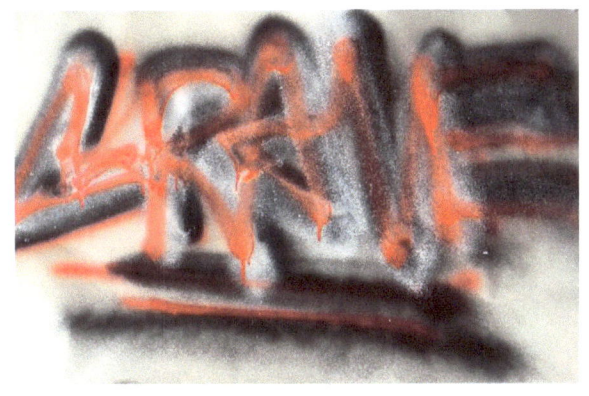

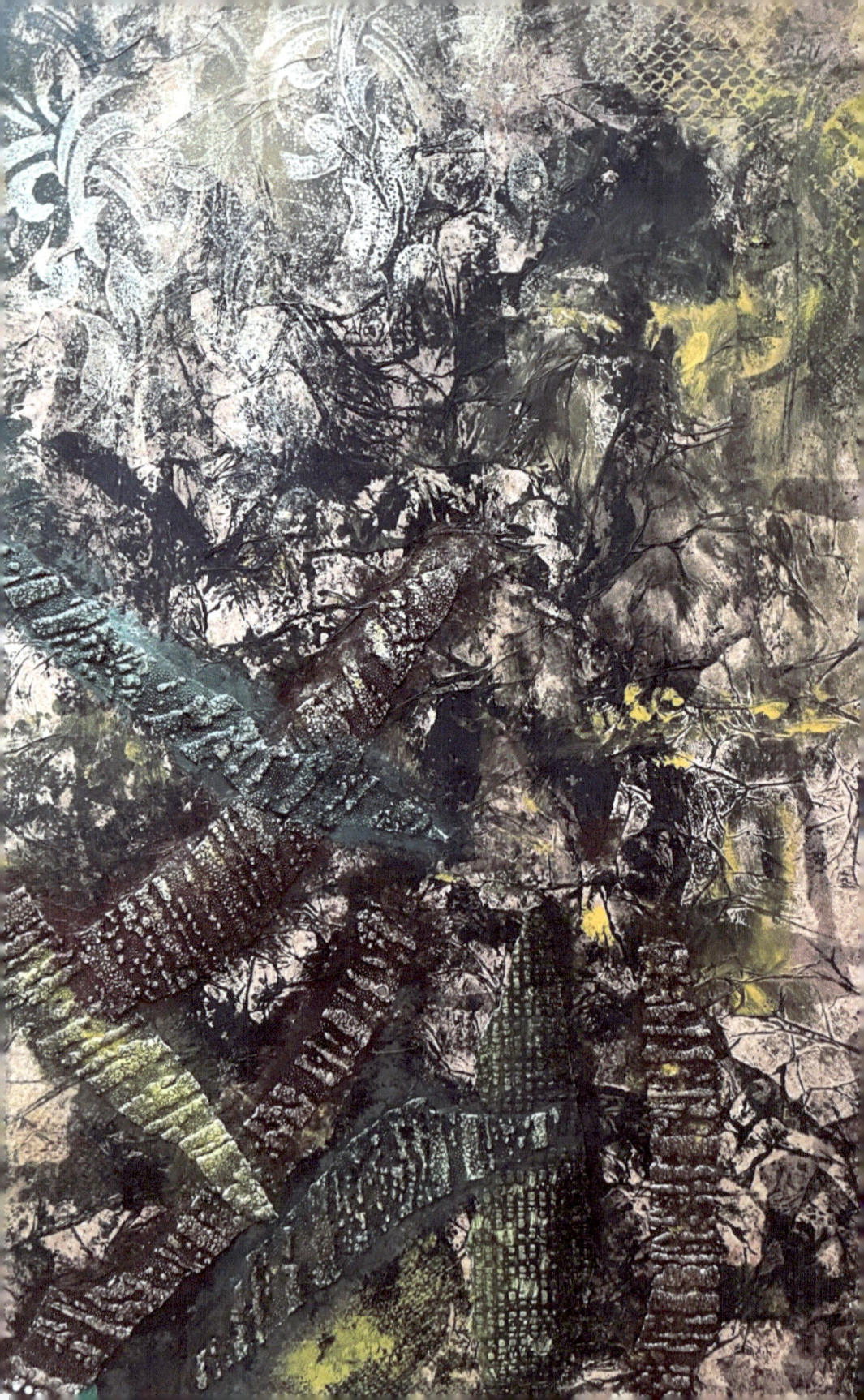

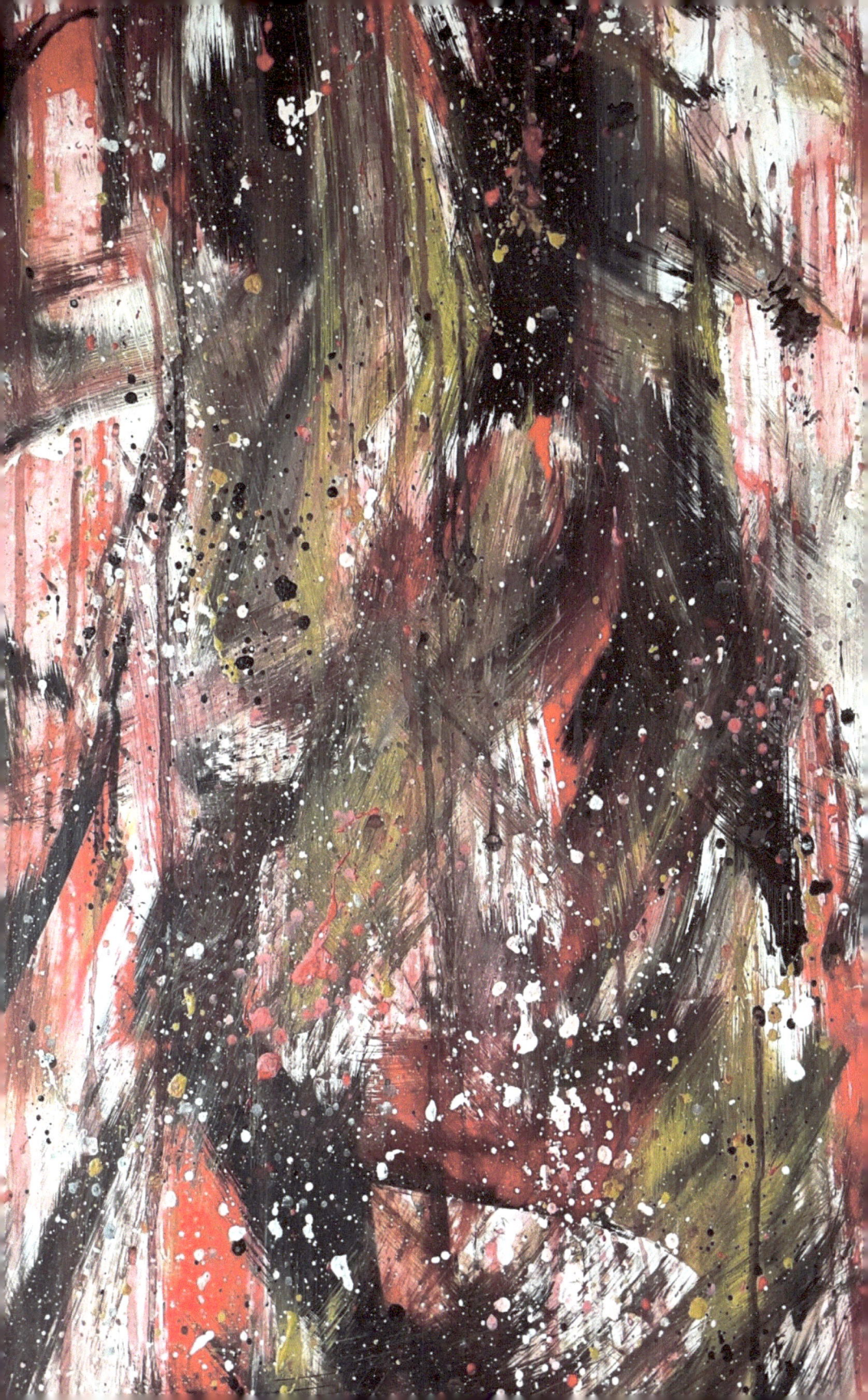

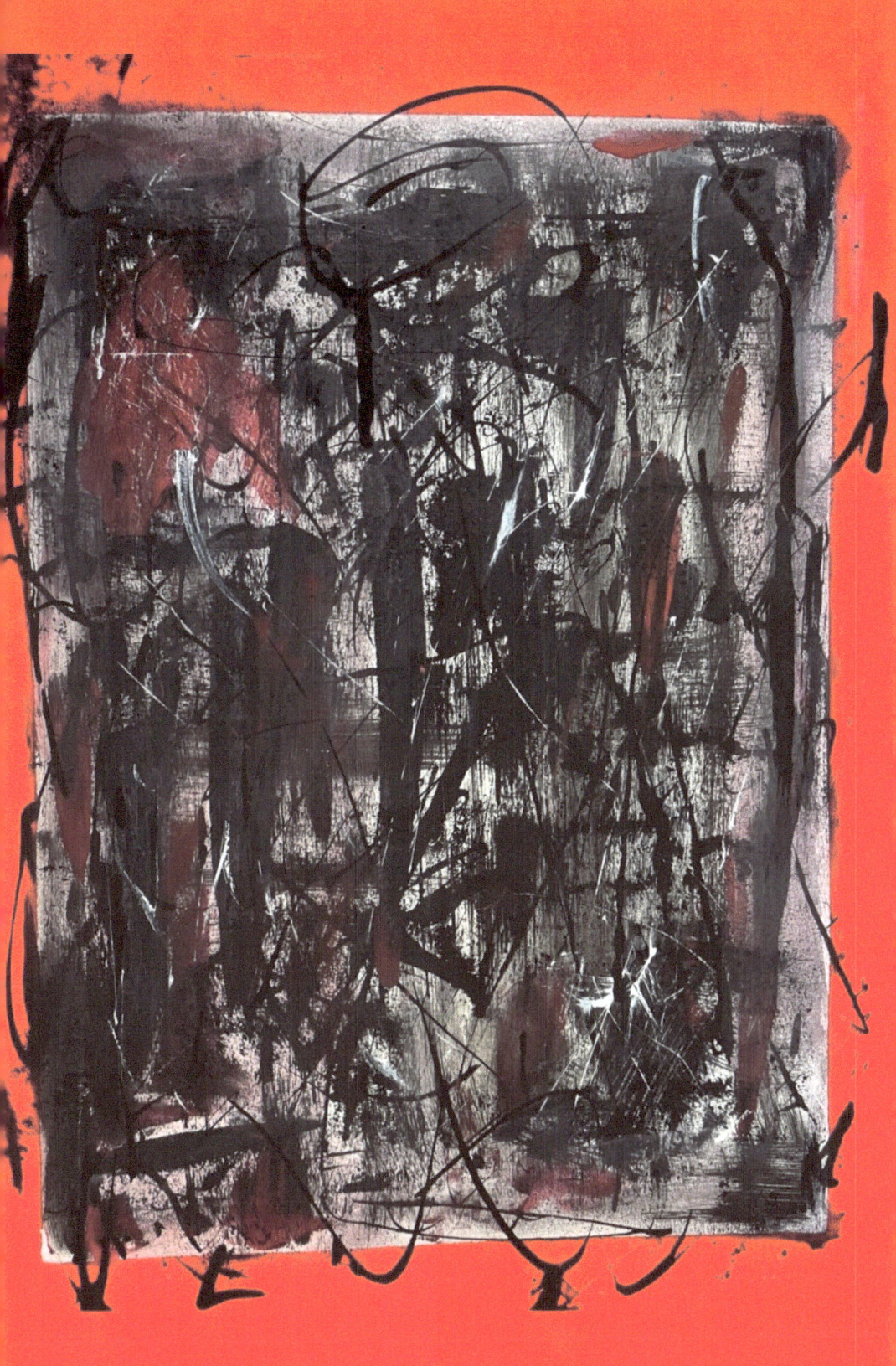

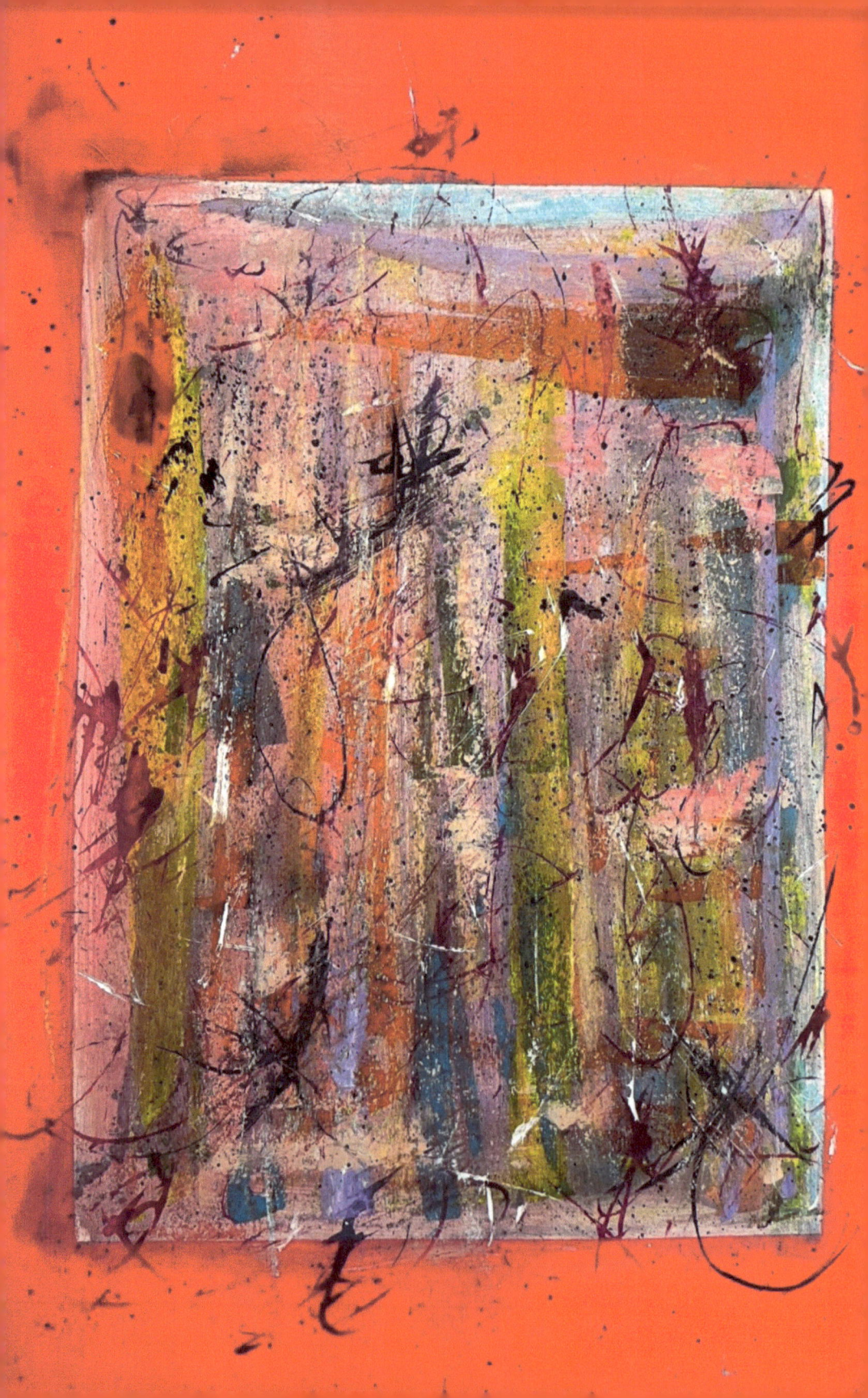

Indie

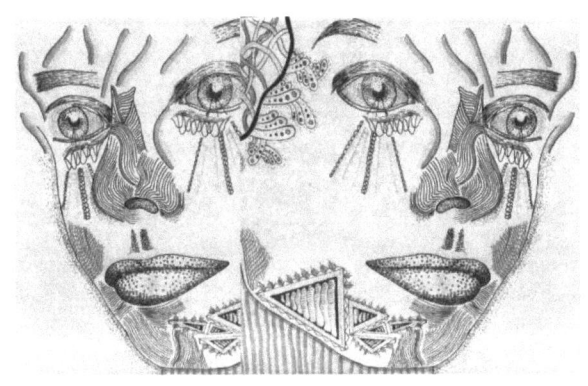

I DON'T KNOW WHO I

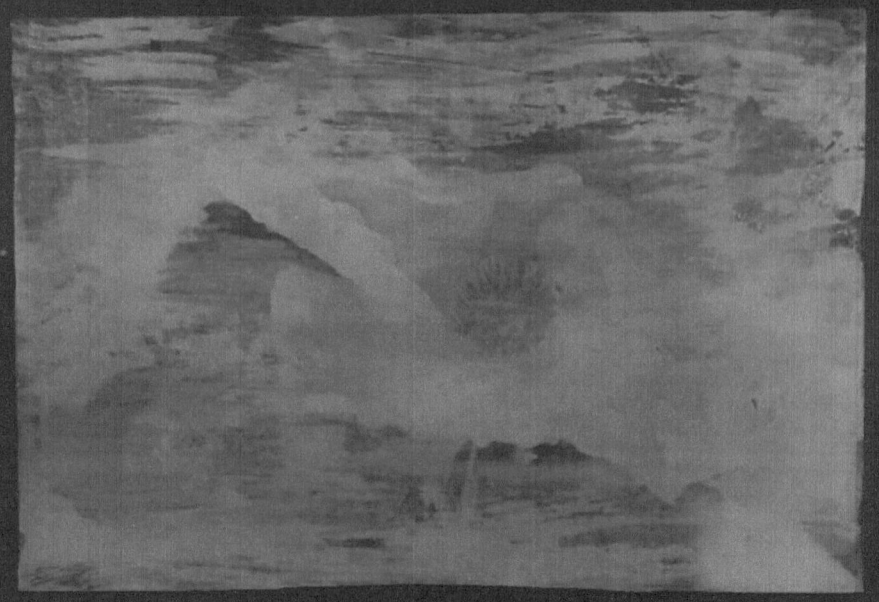

AM ANYMORE

I'VE NEVER FELT LIKE

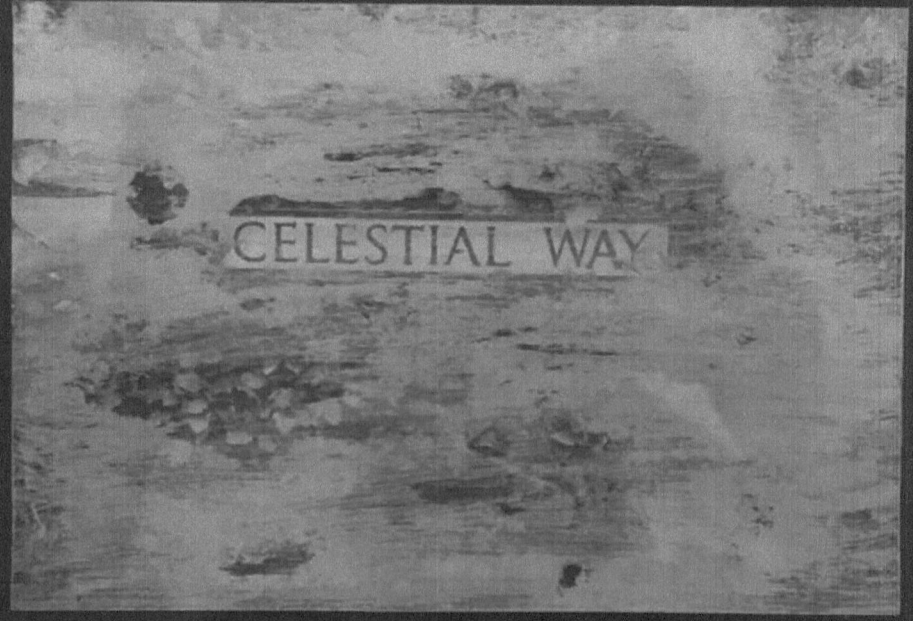

THIS BEFORE

I DON'T WANT

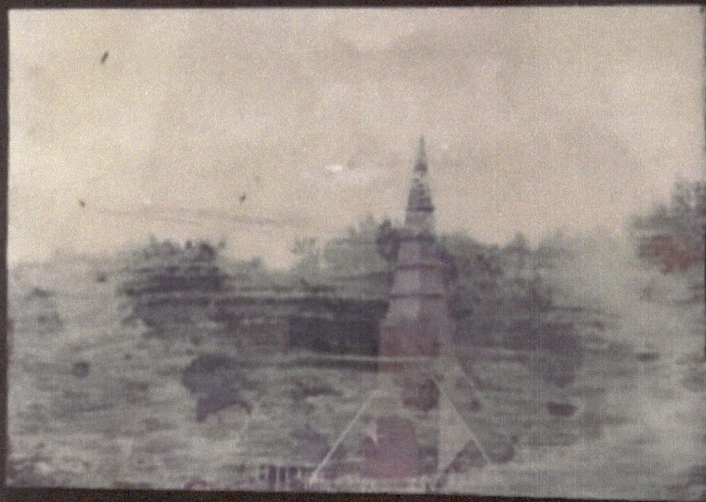

TO LOSE YOU

IT GETS LONELY UP

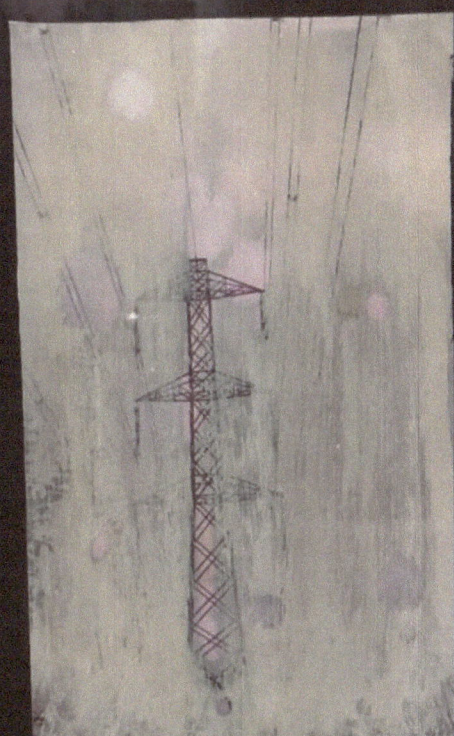

HERE SOMETIMES

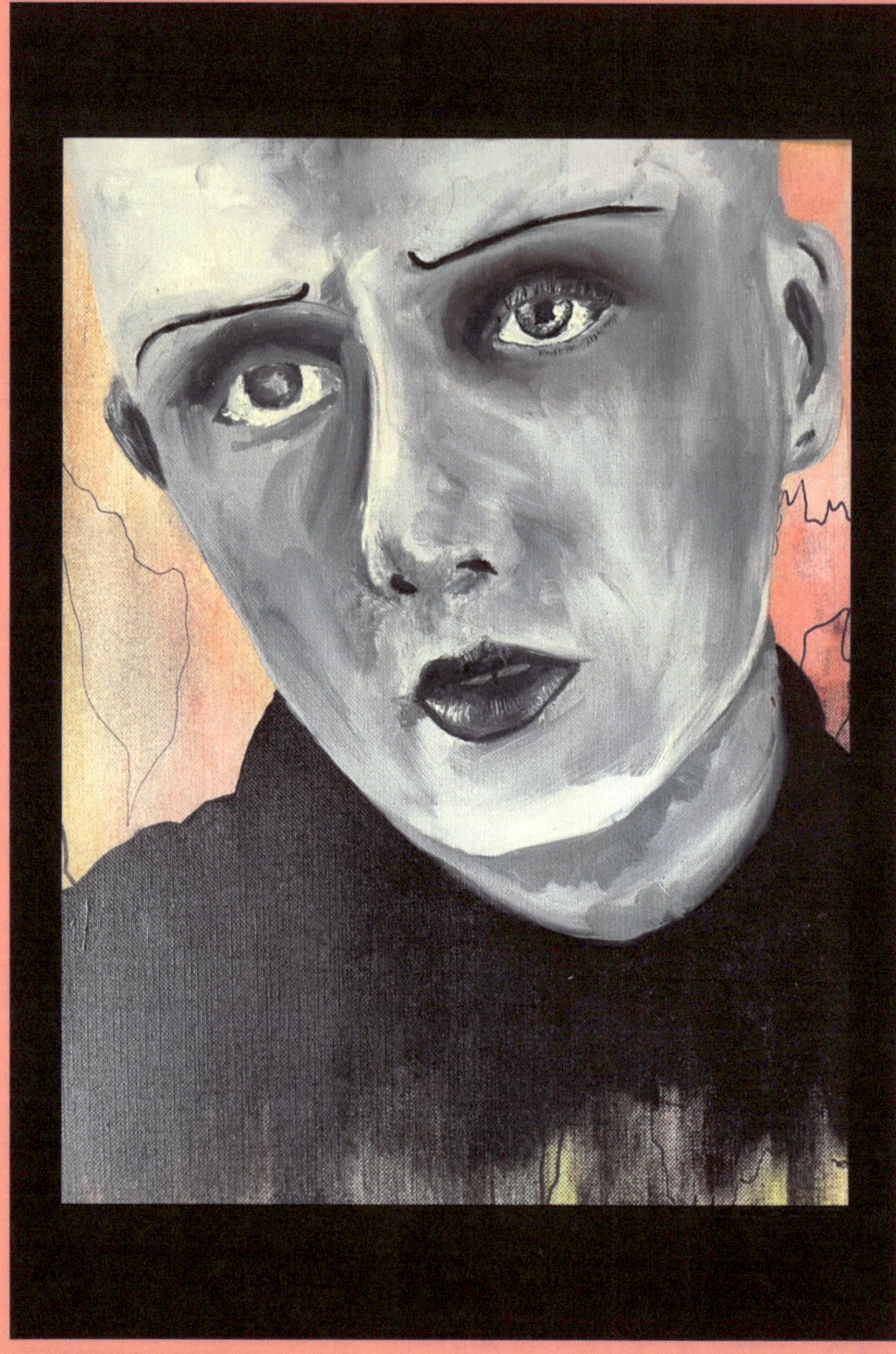

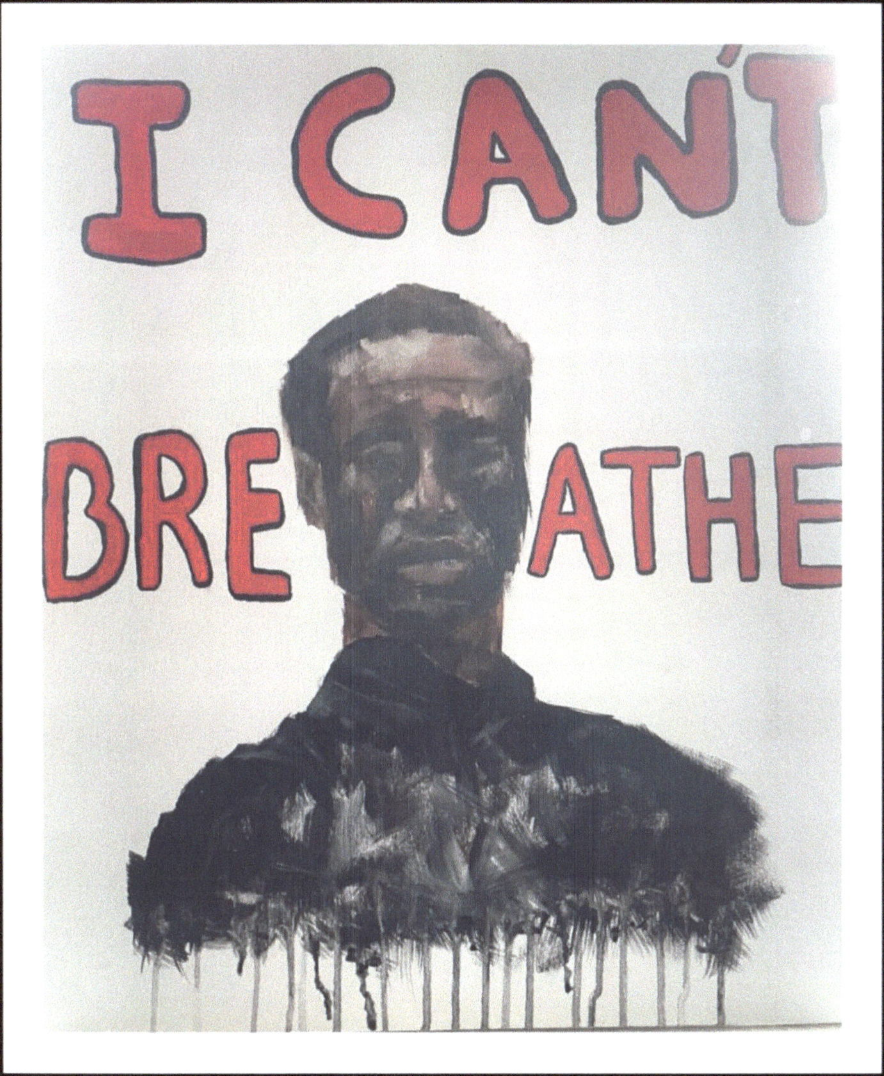
I CAN'T
BRE ATHE

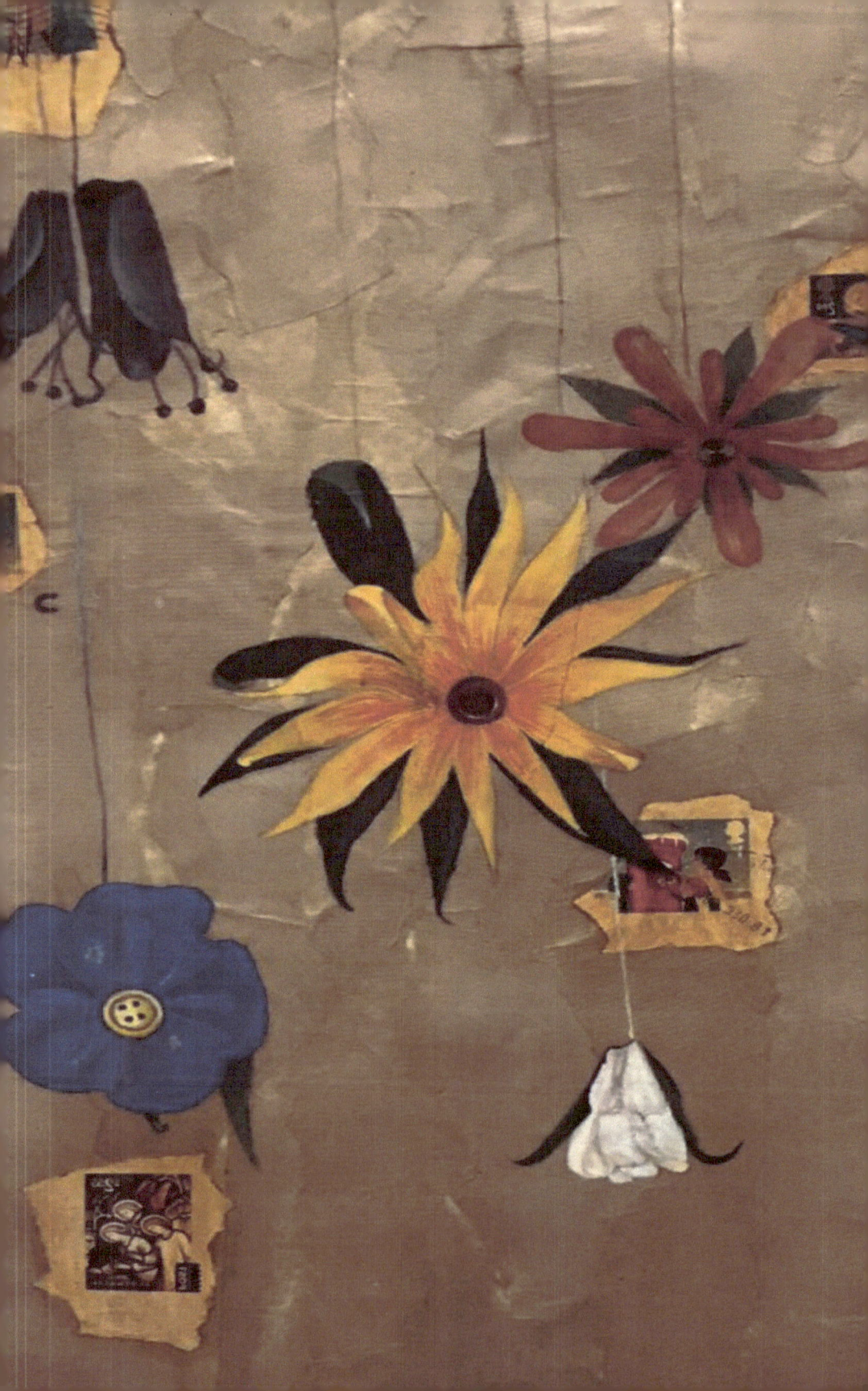

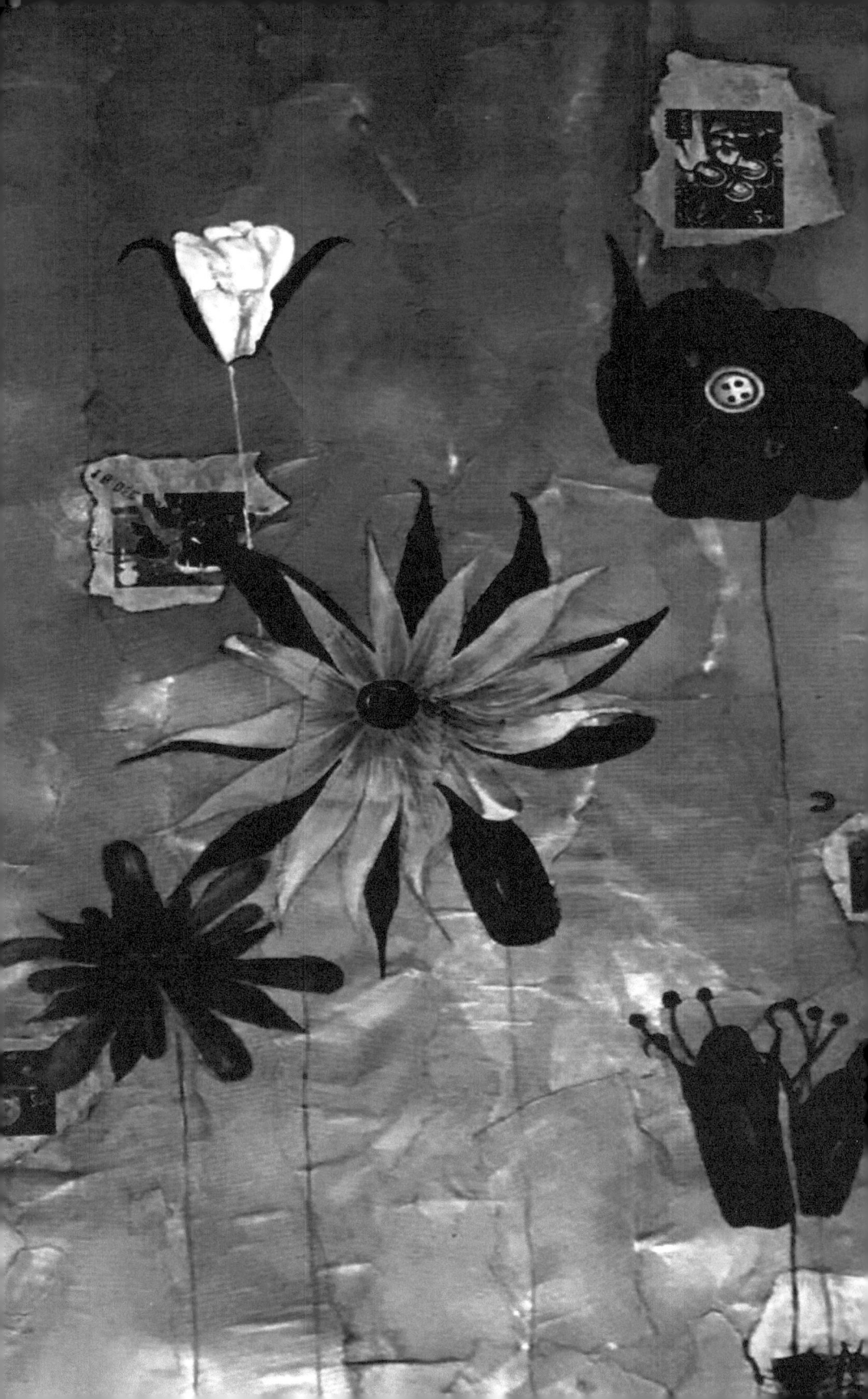

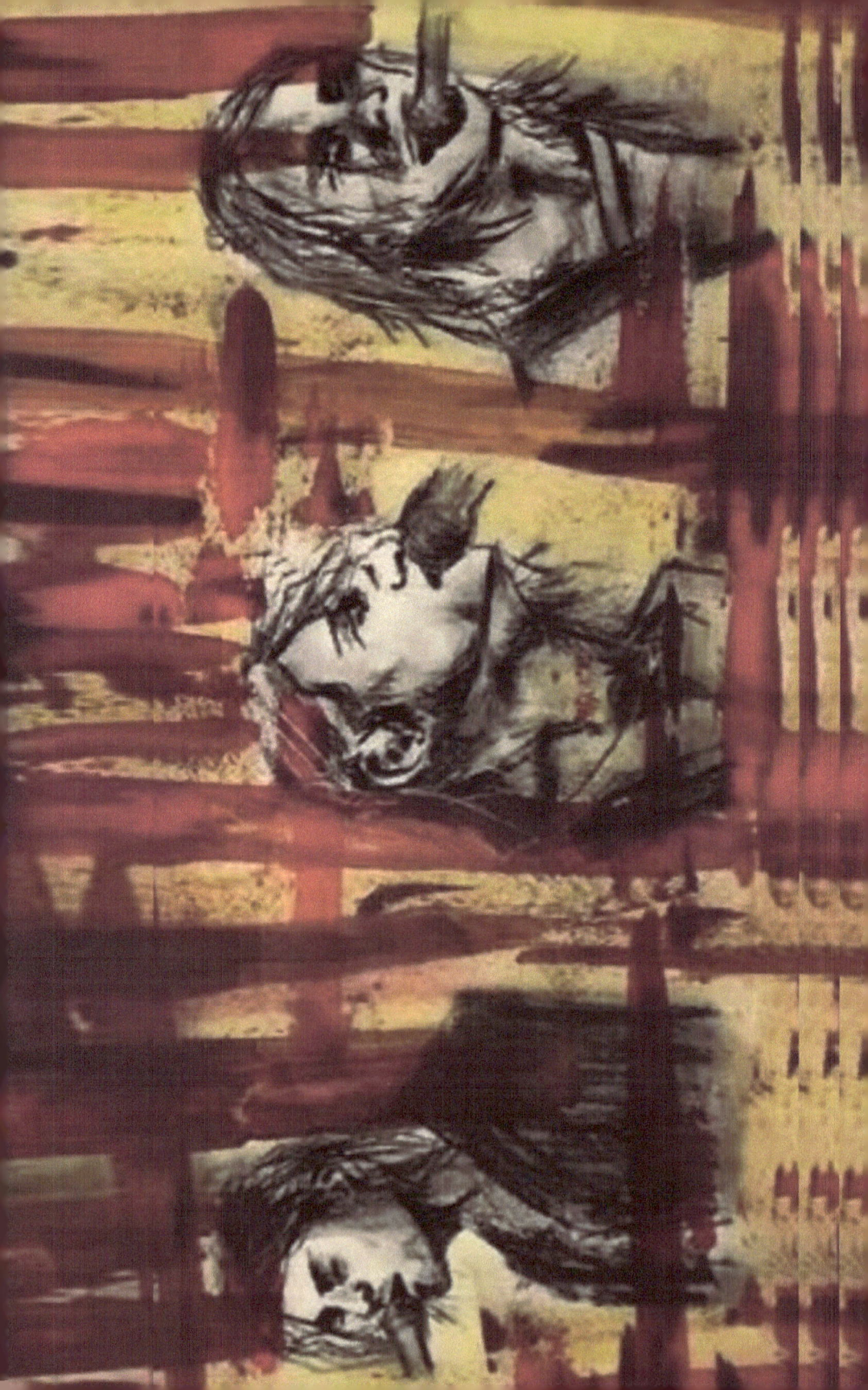

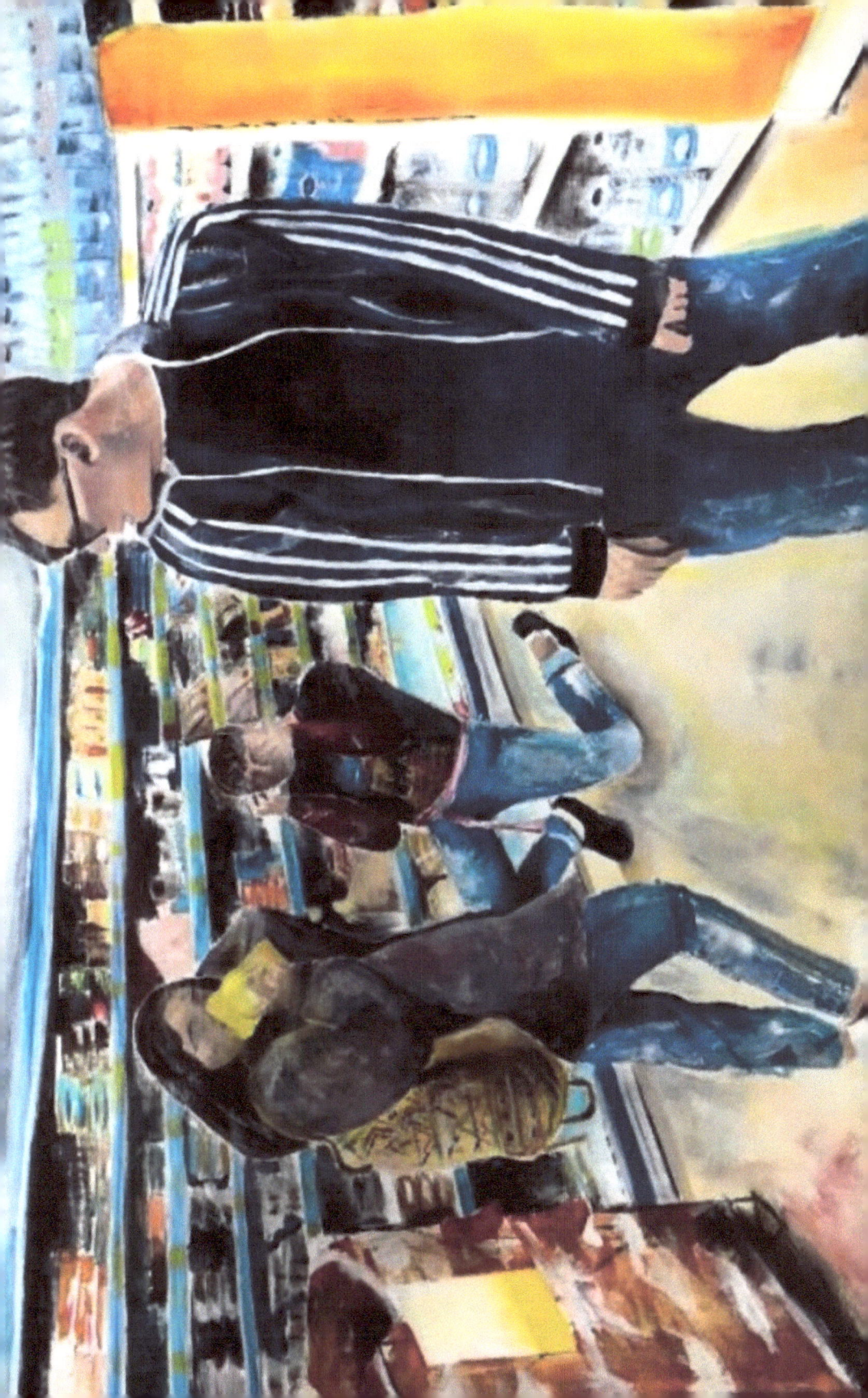

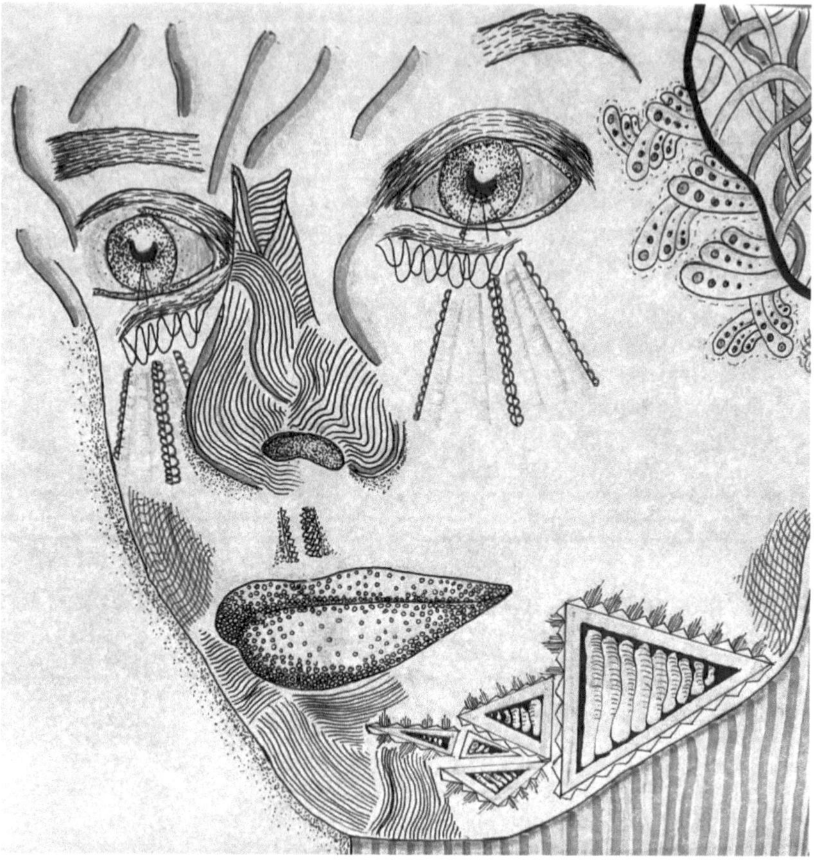

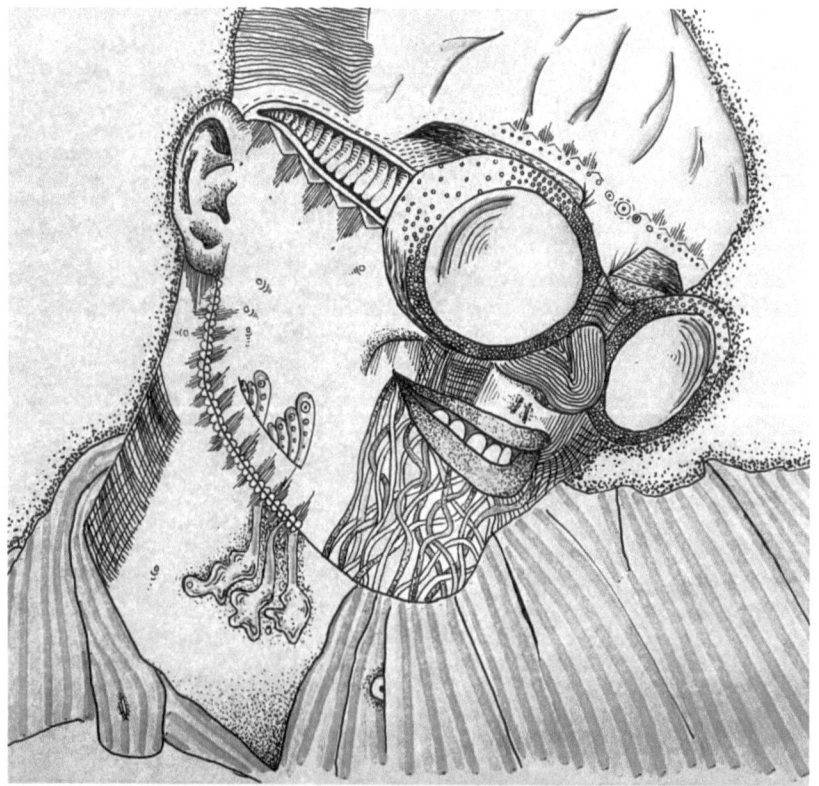

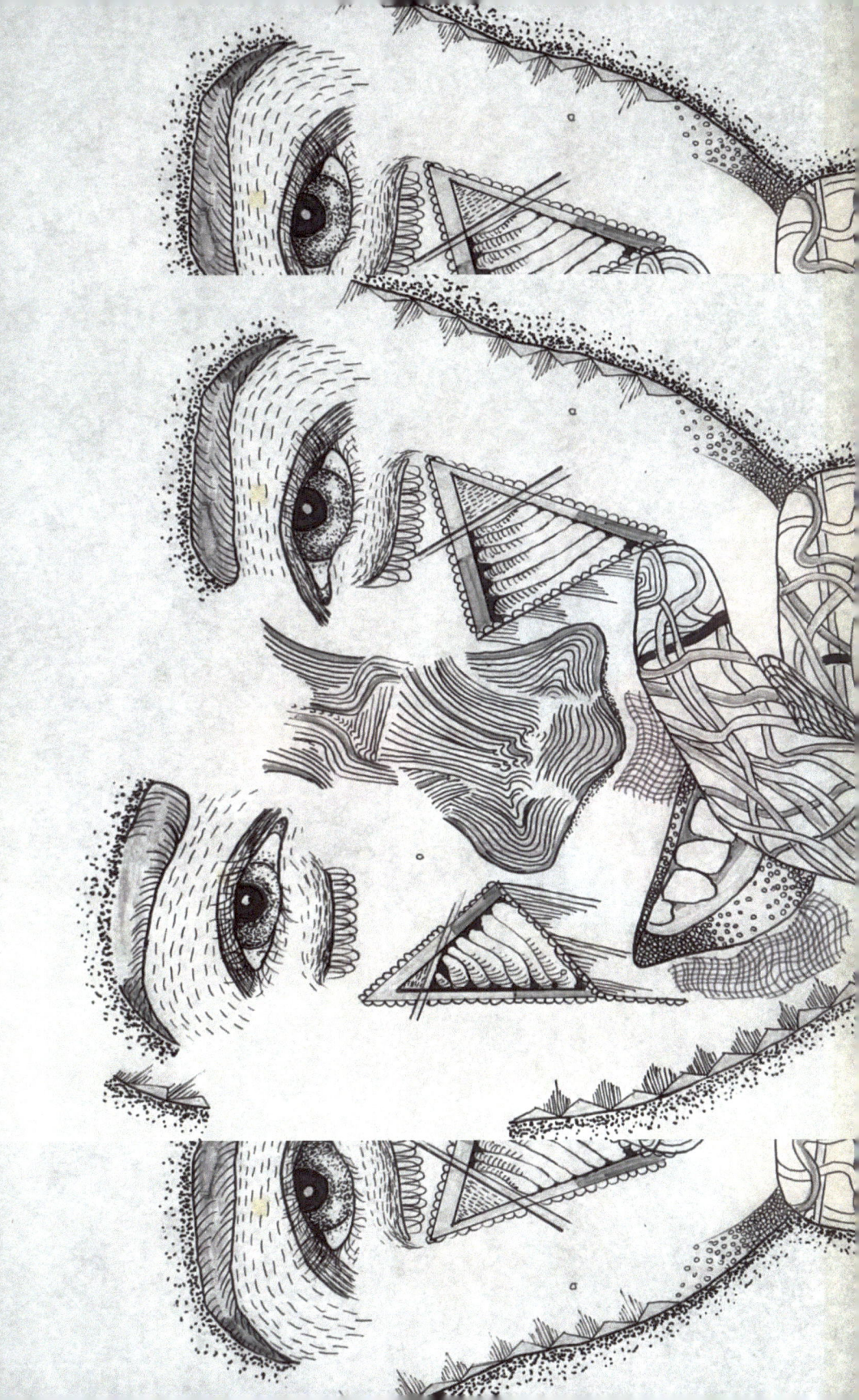

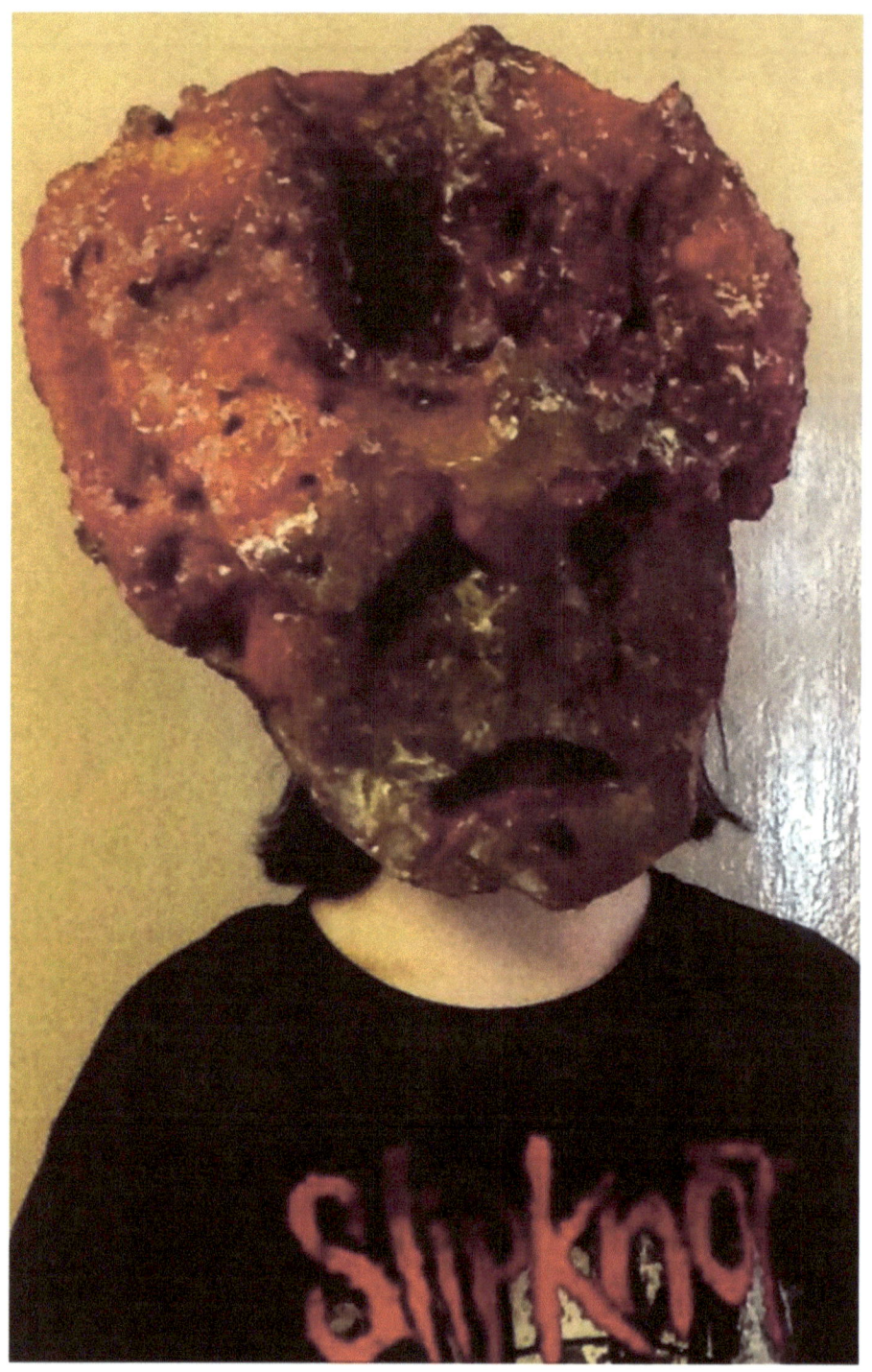

Still Life

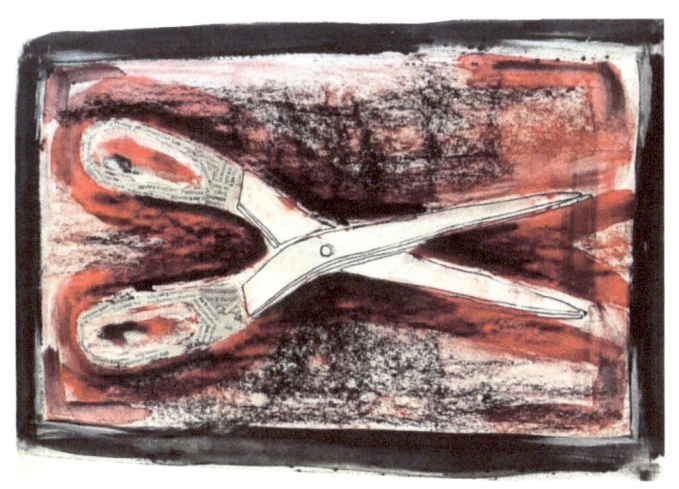

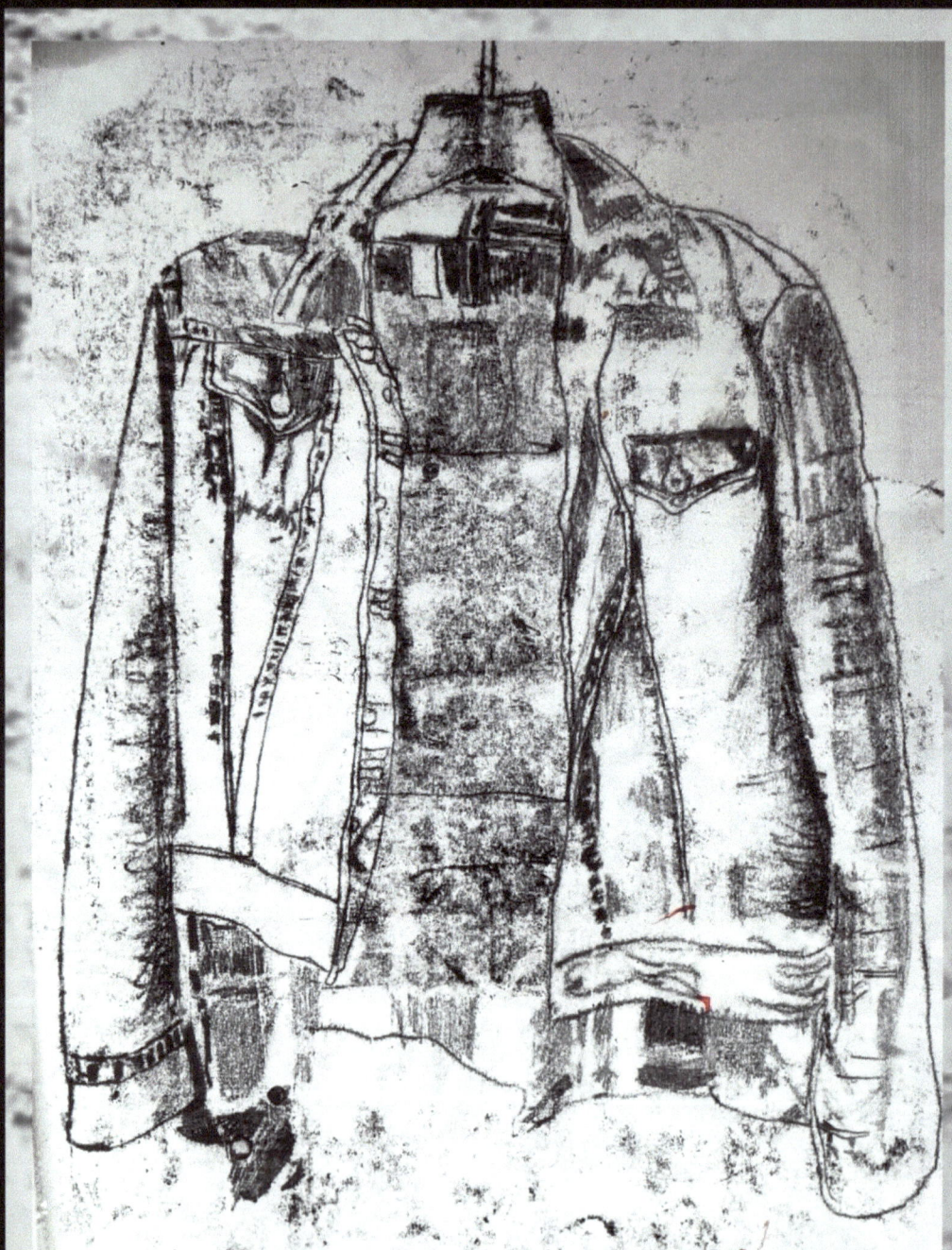

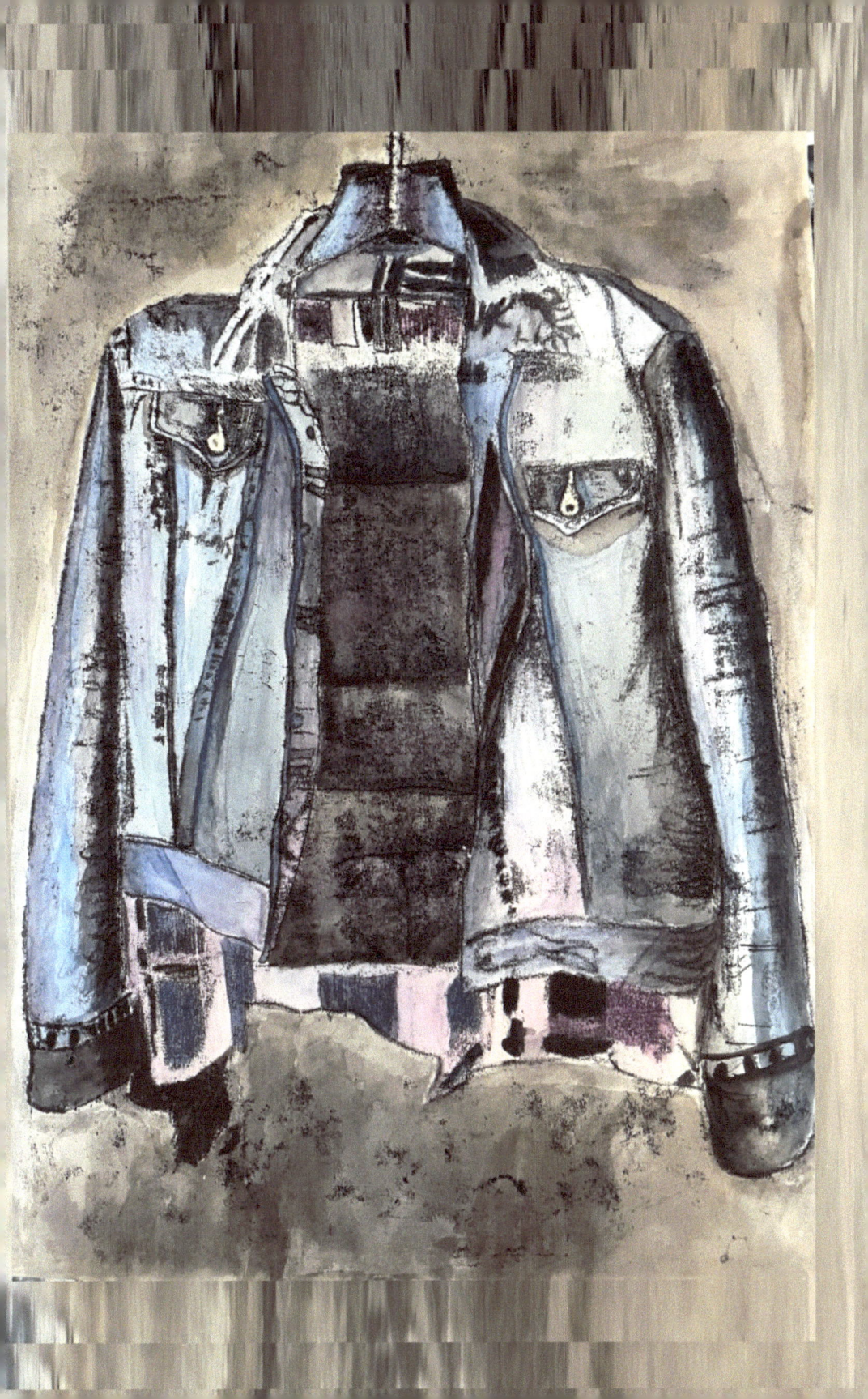

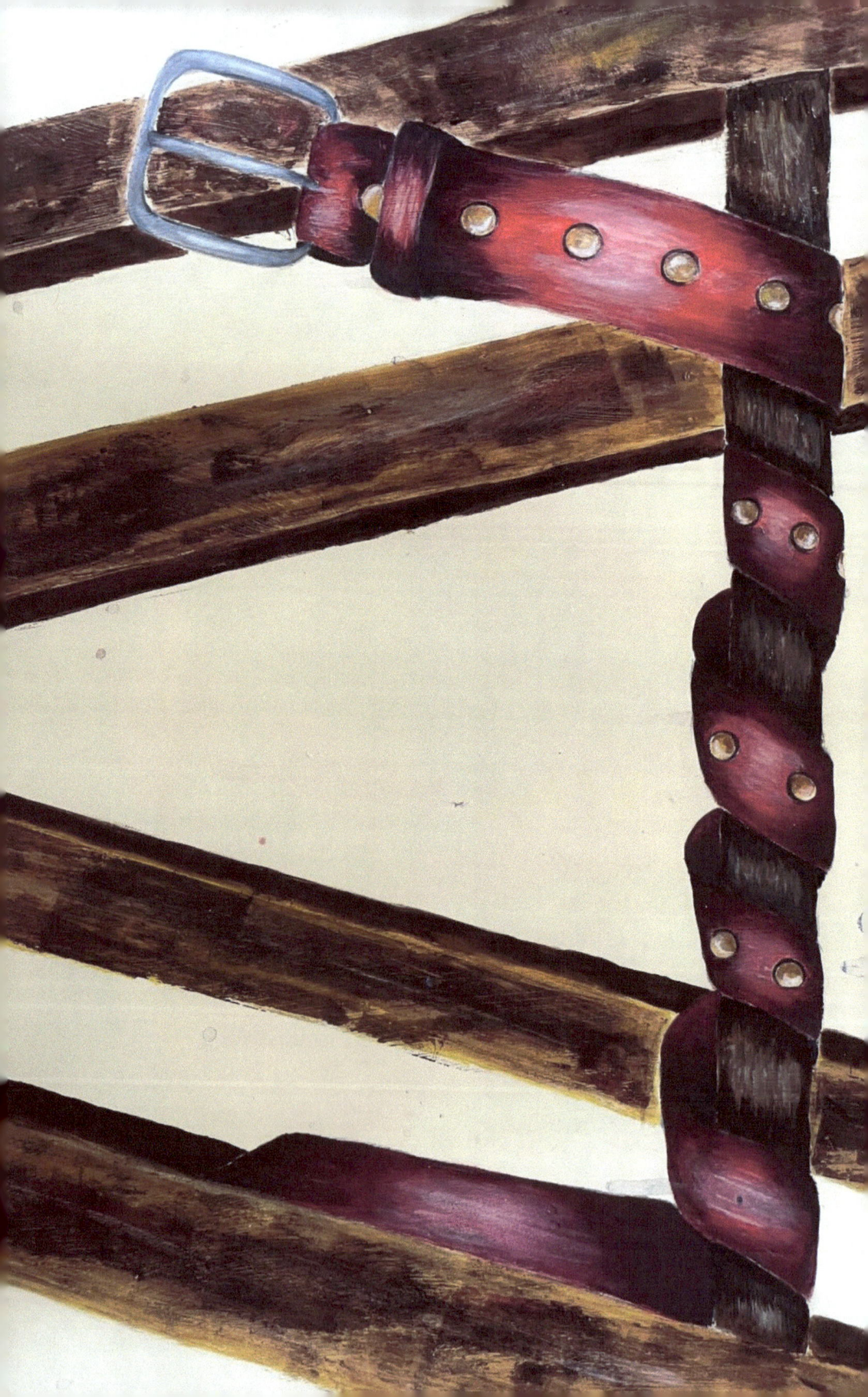

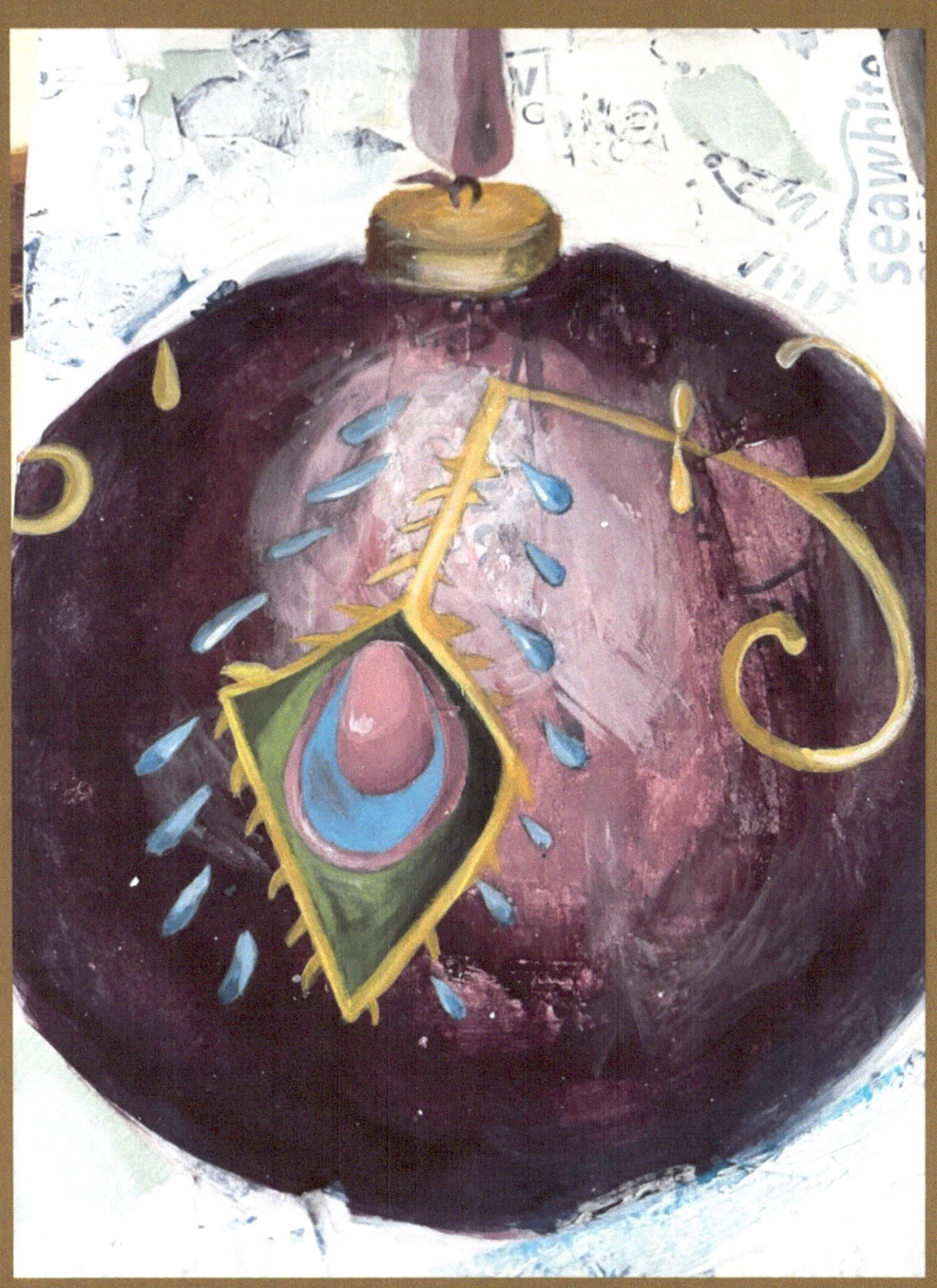

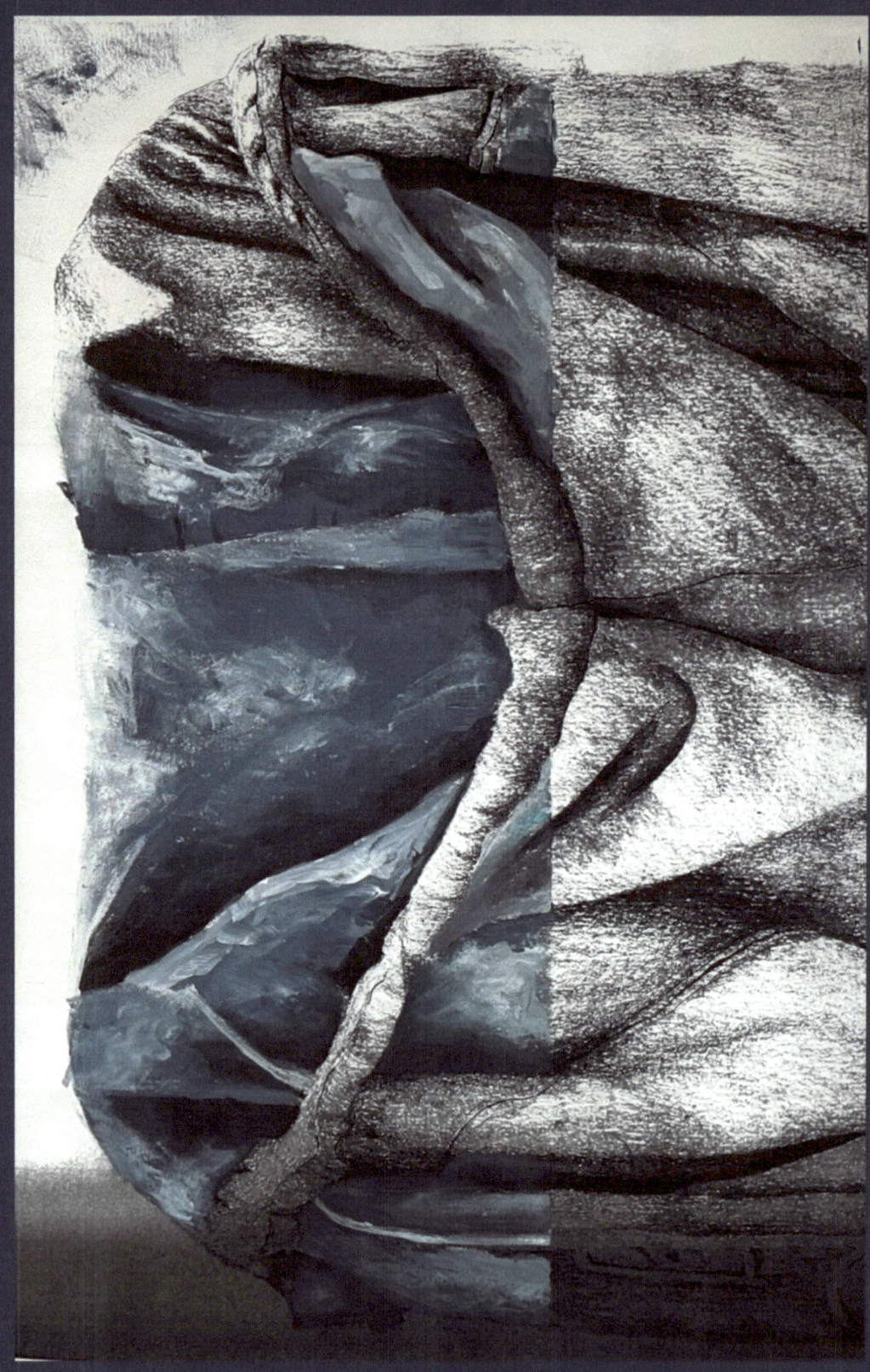

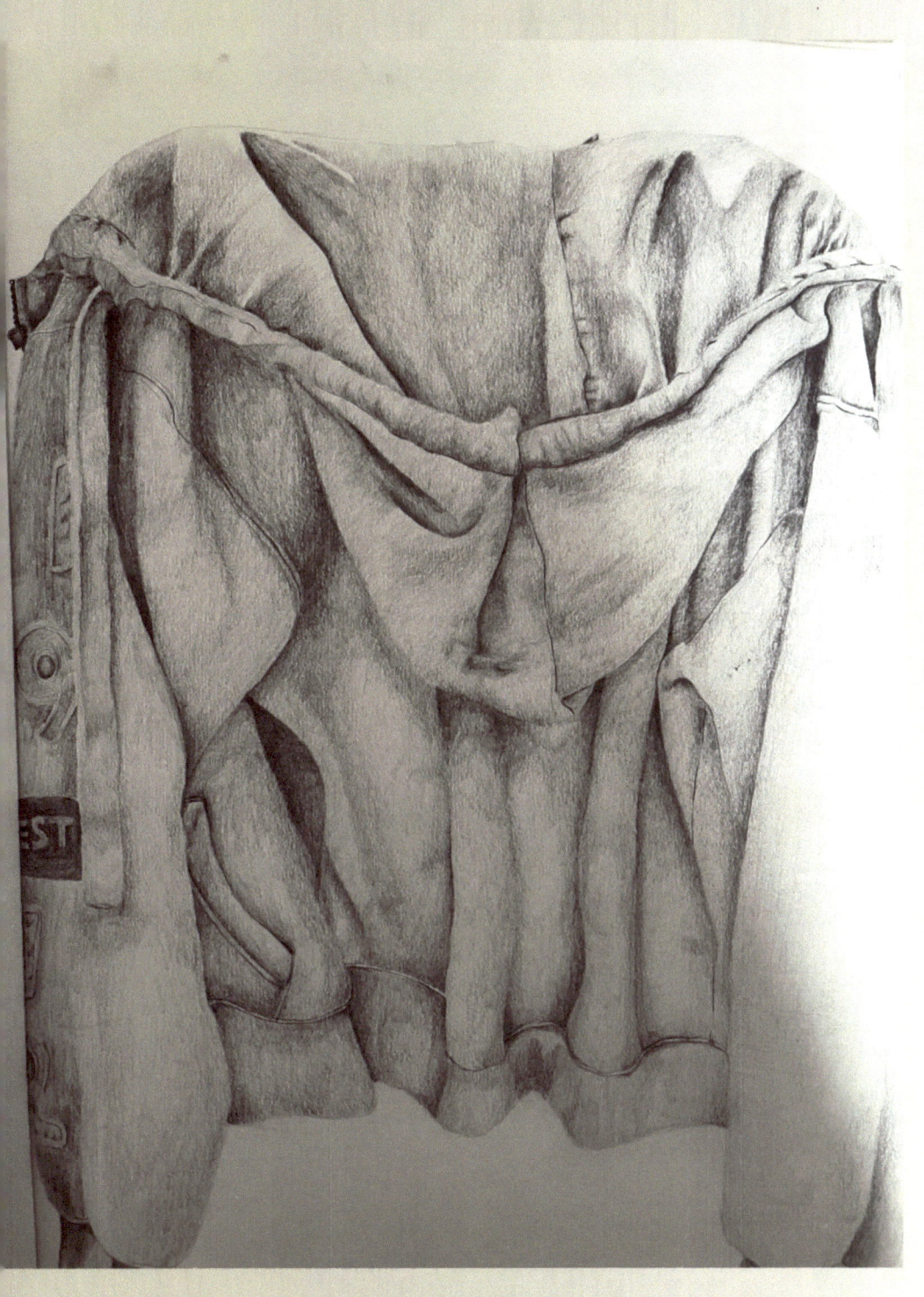

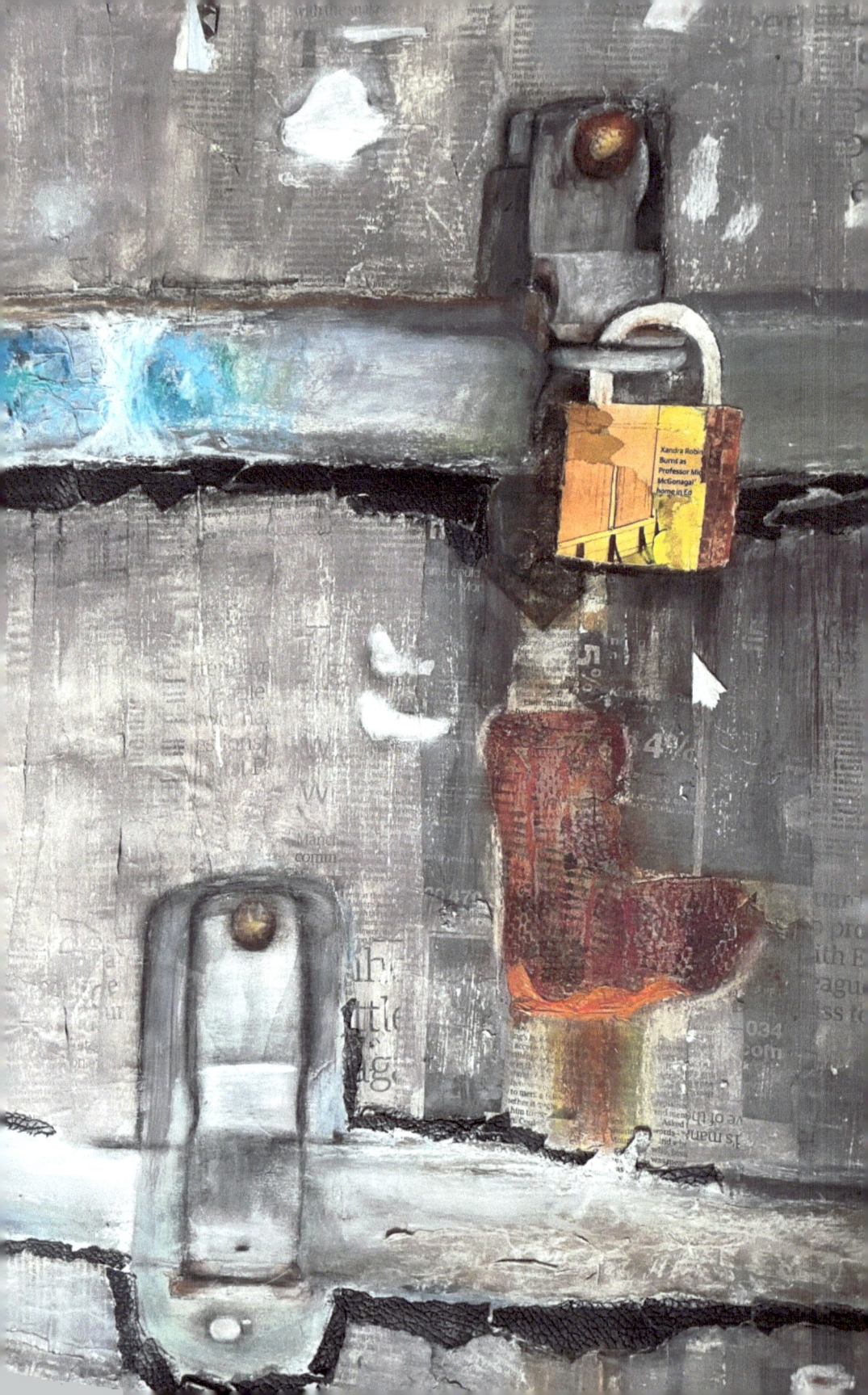

Life

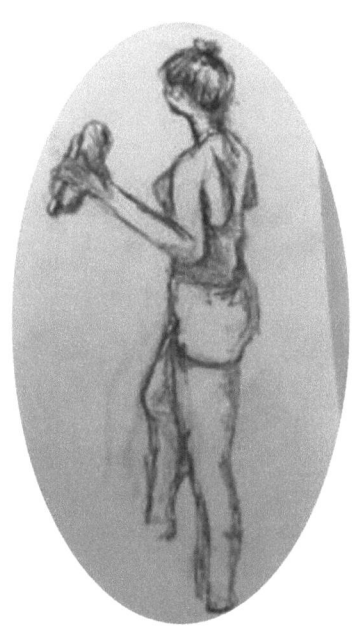

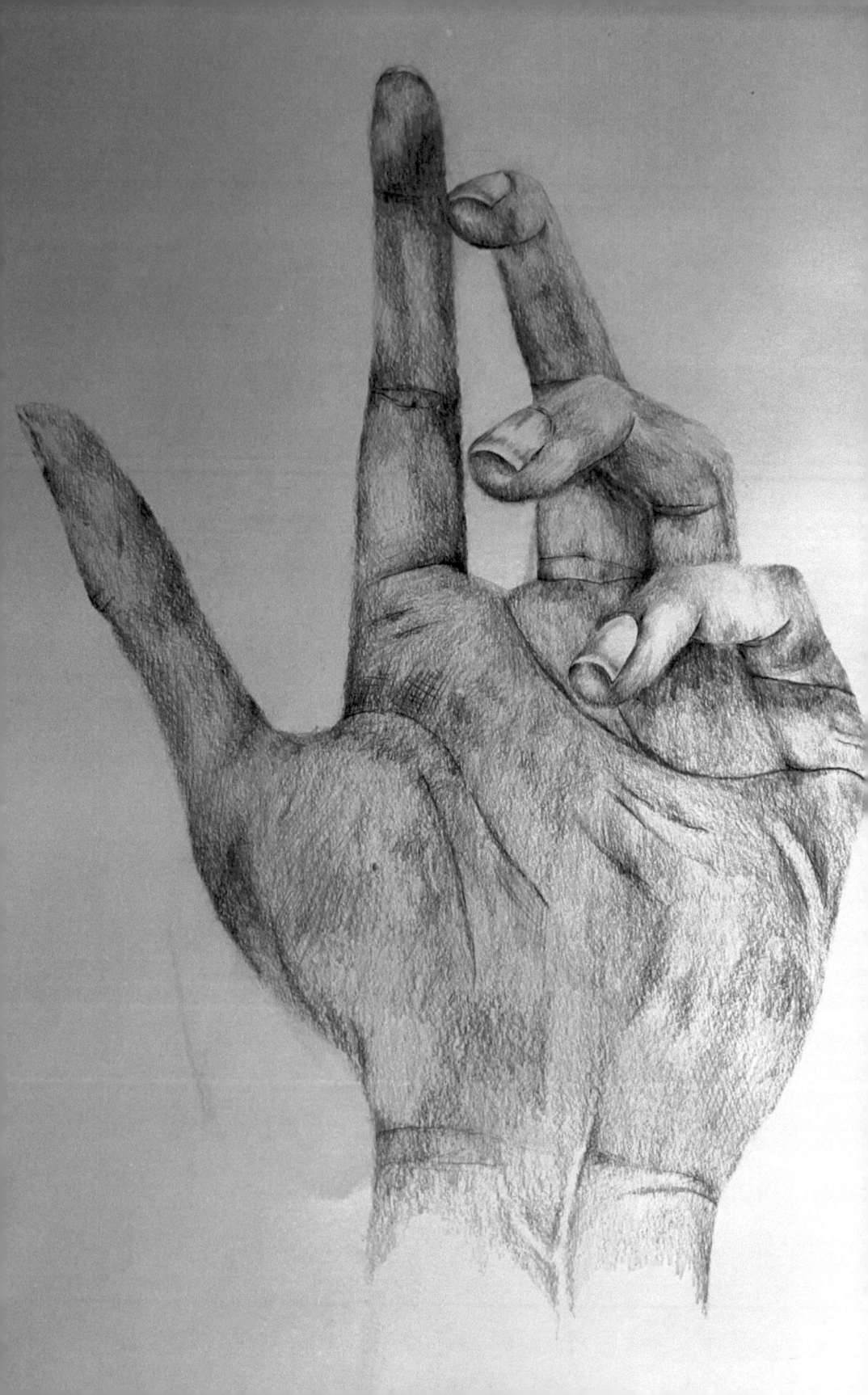

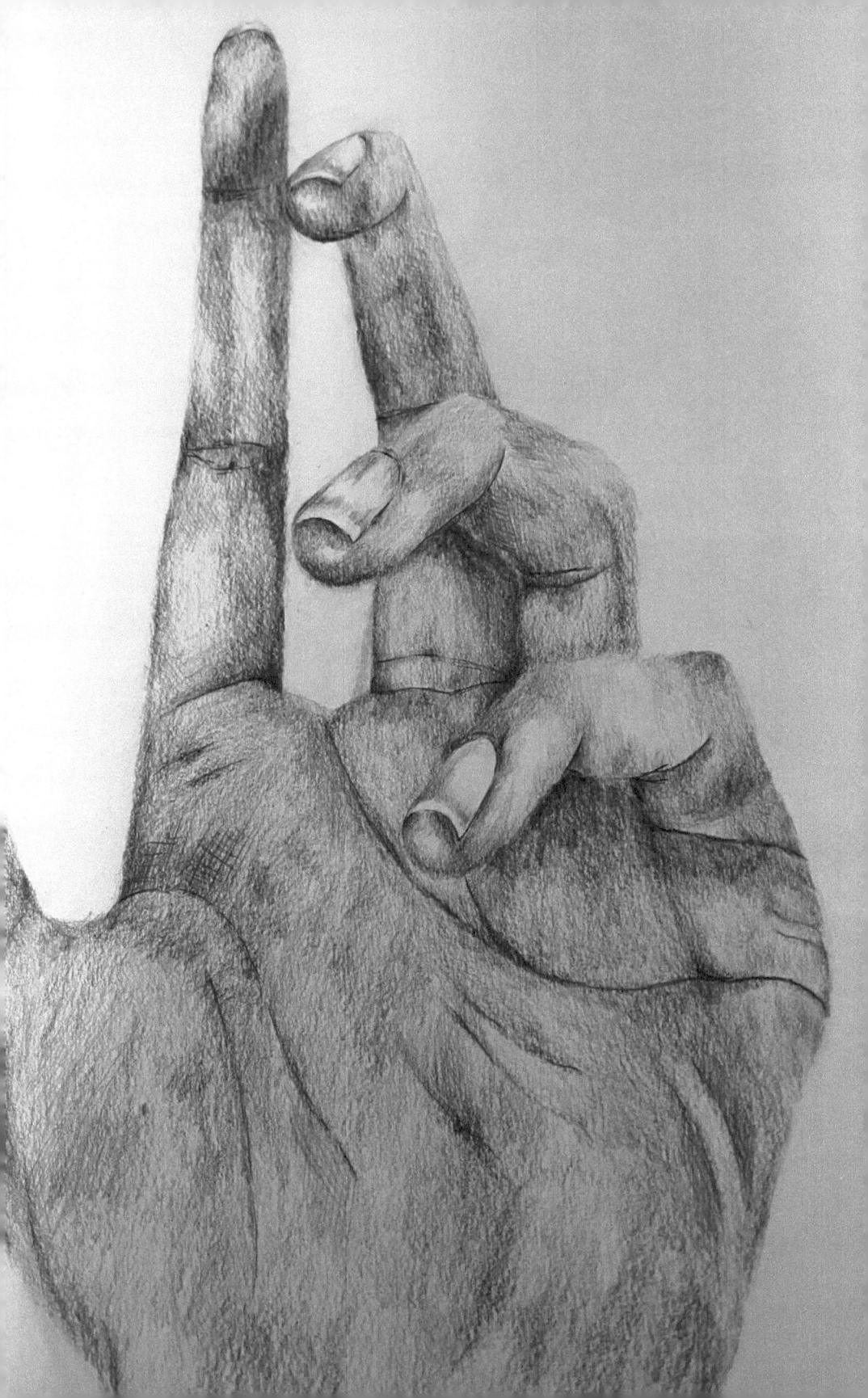

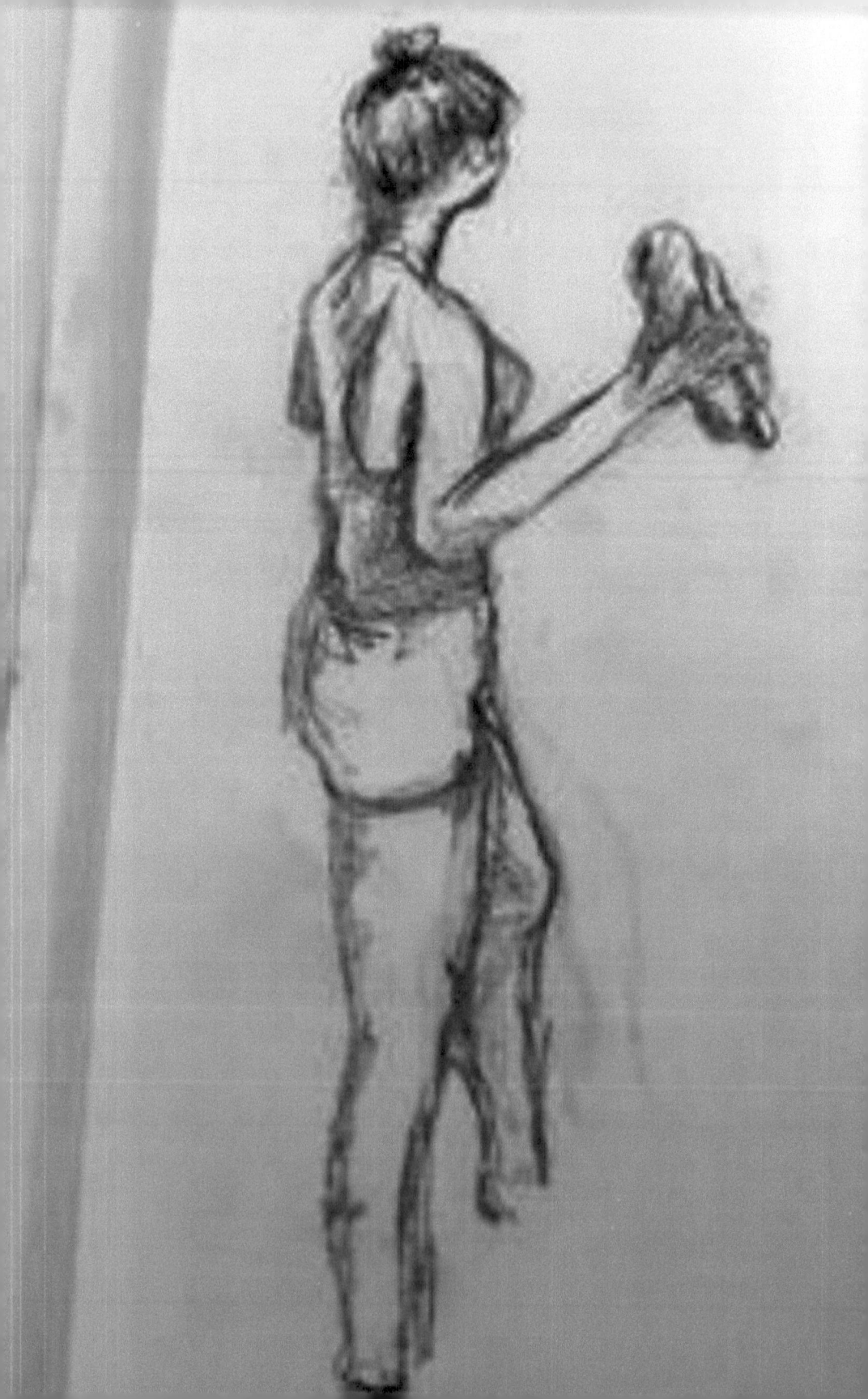

Nature

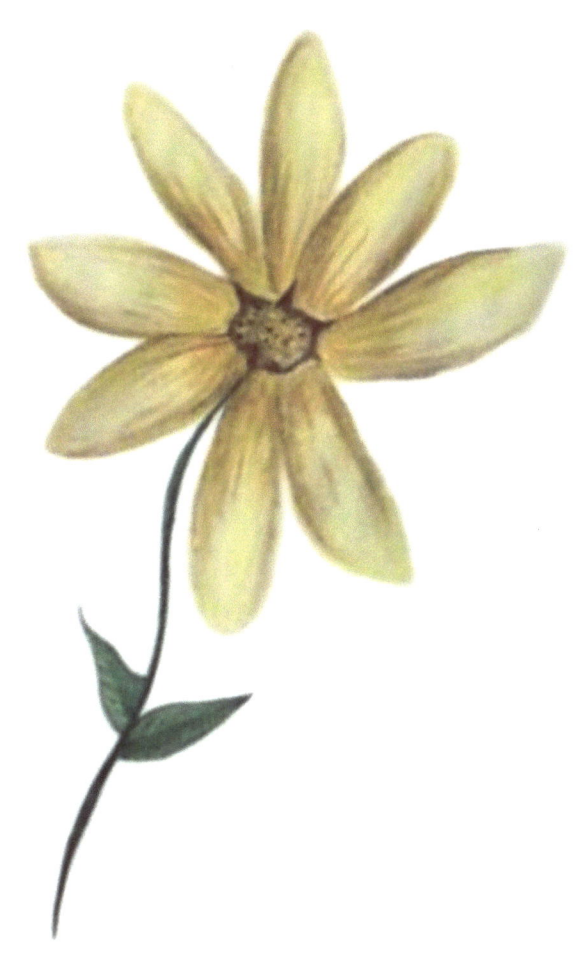

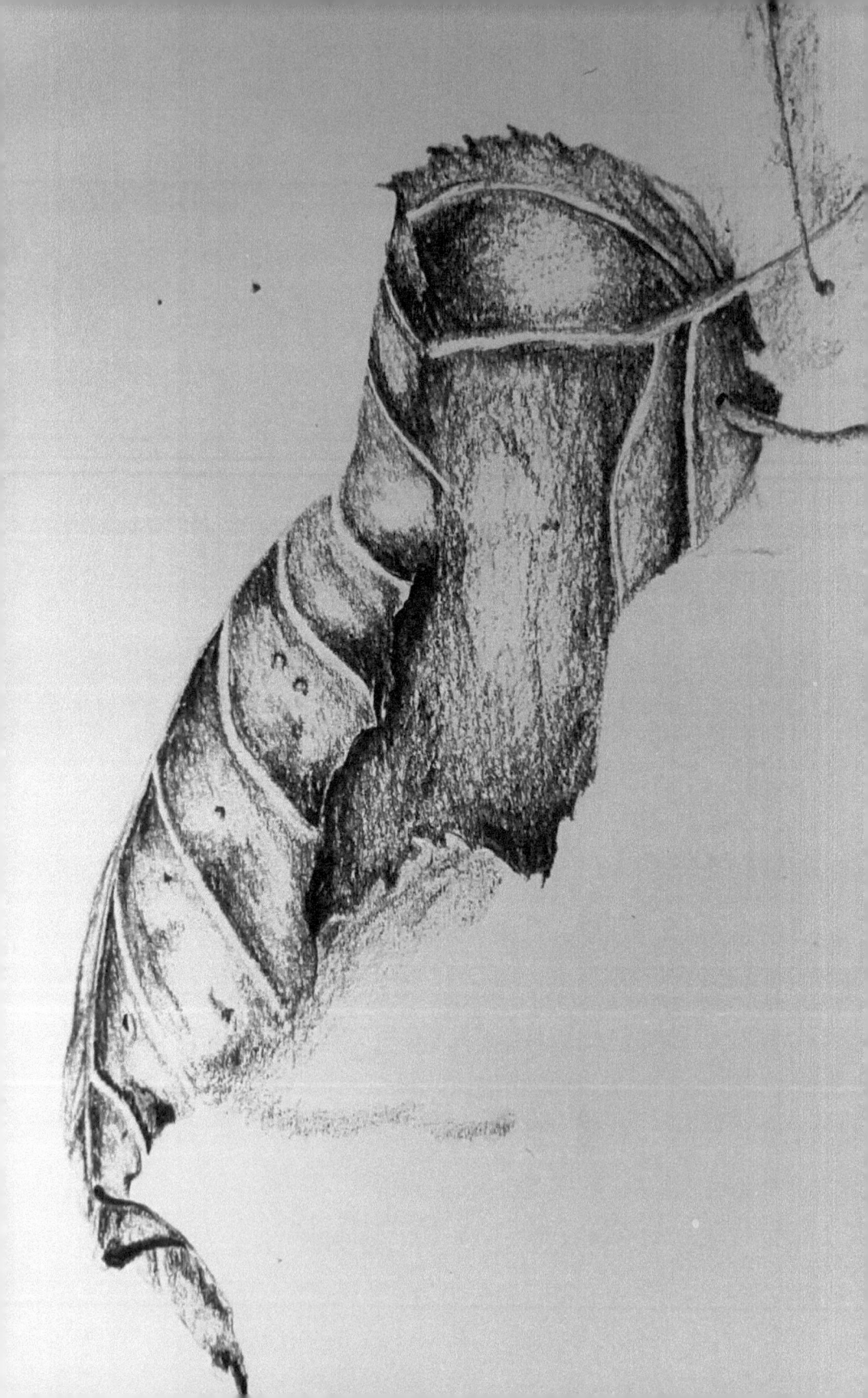

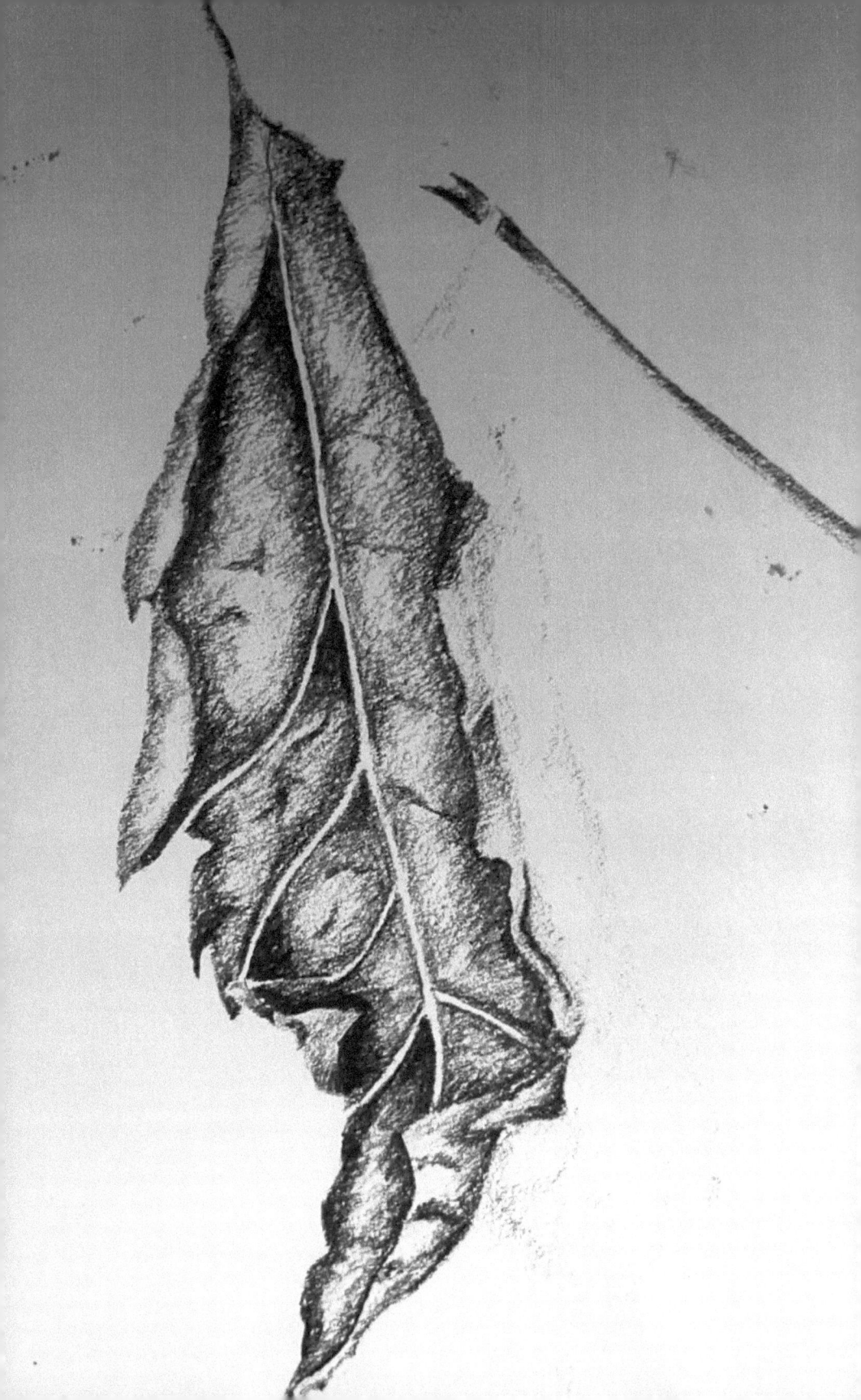

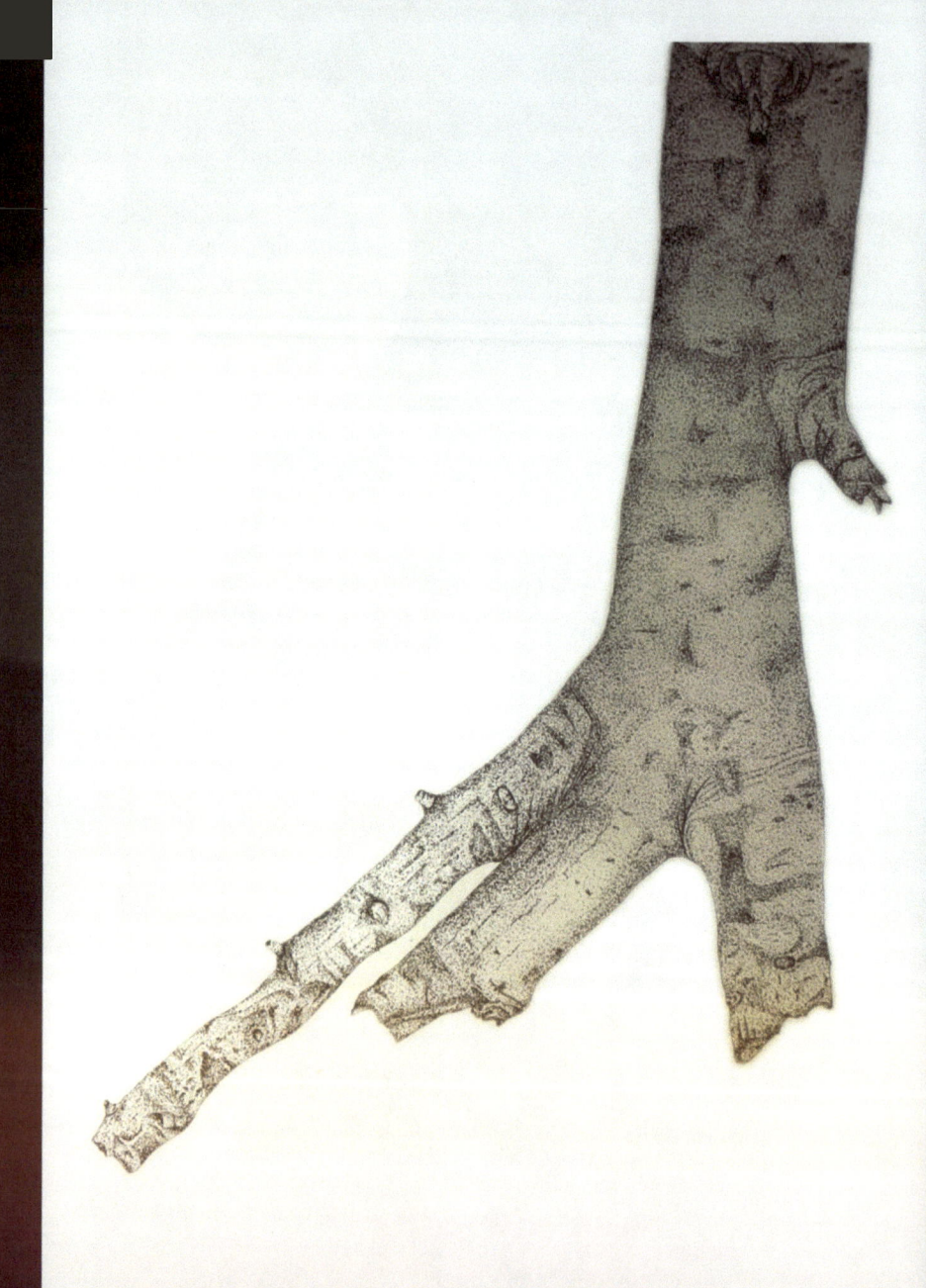

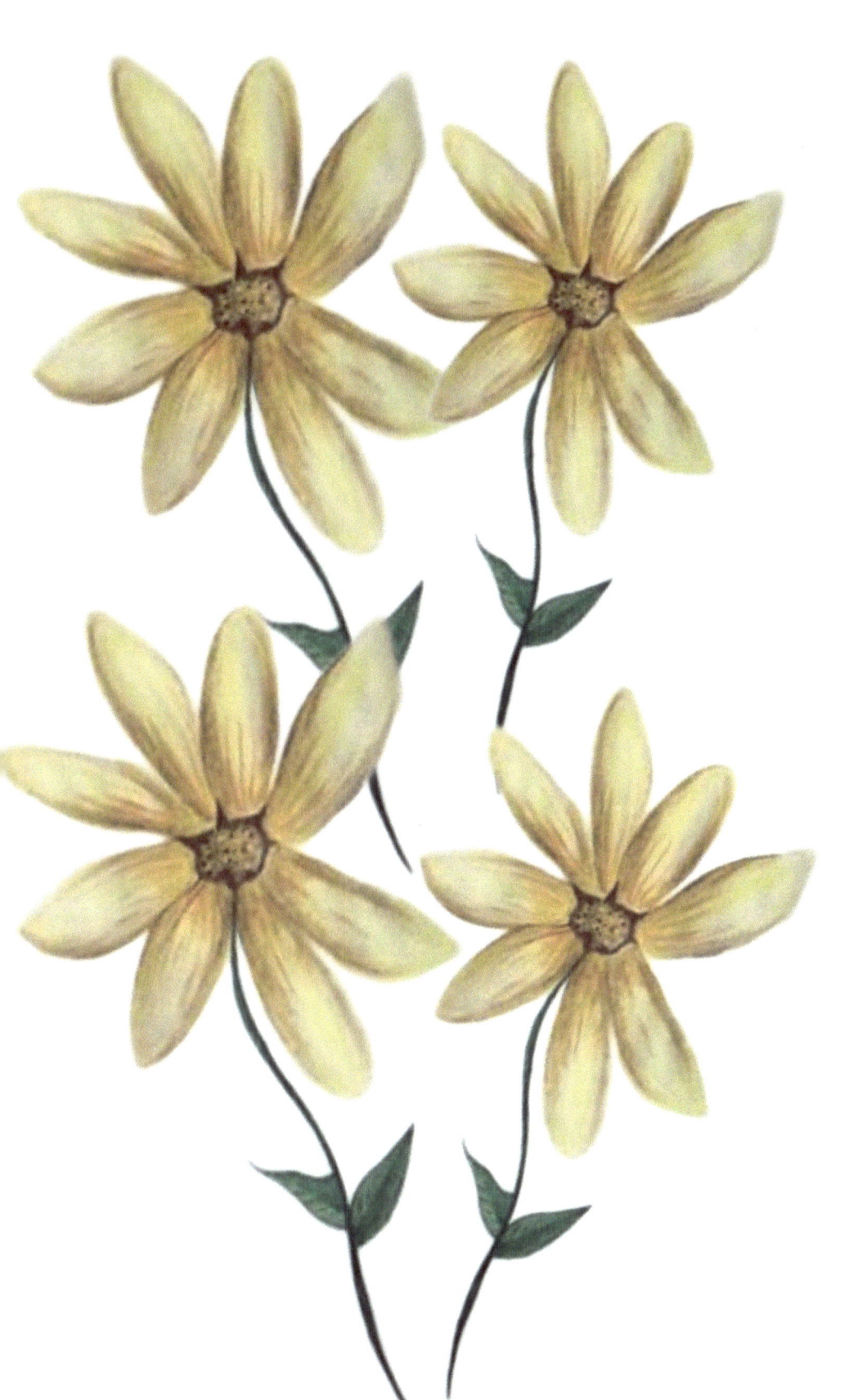

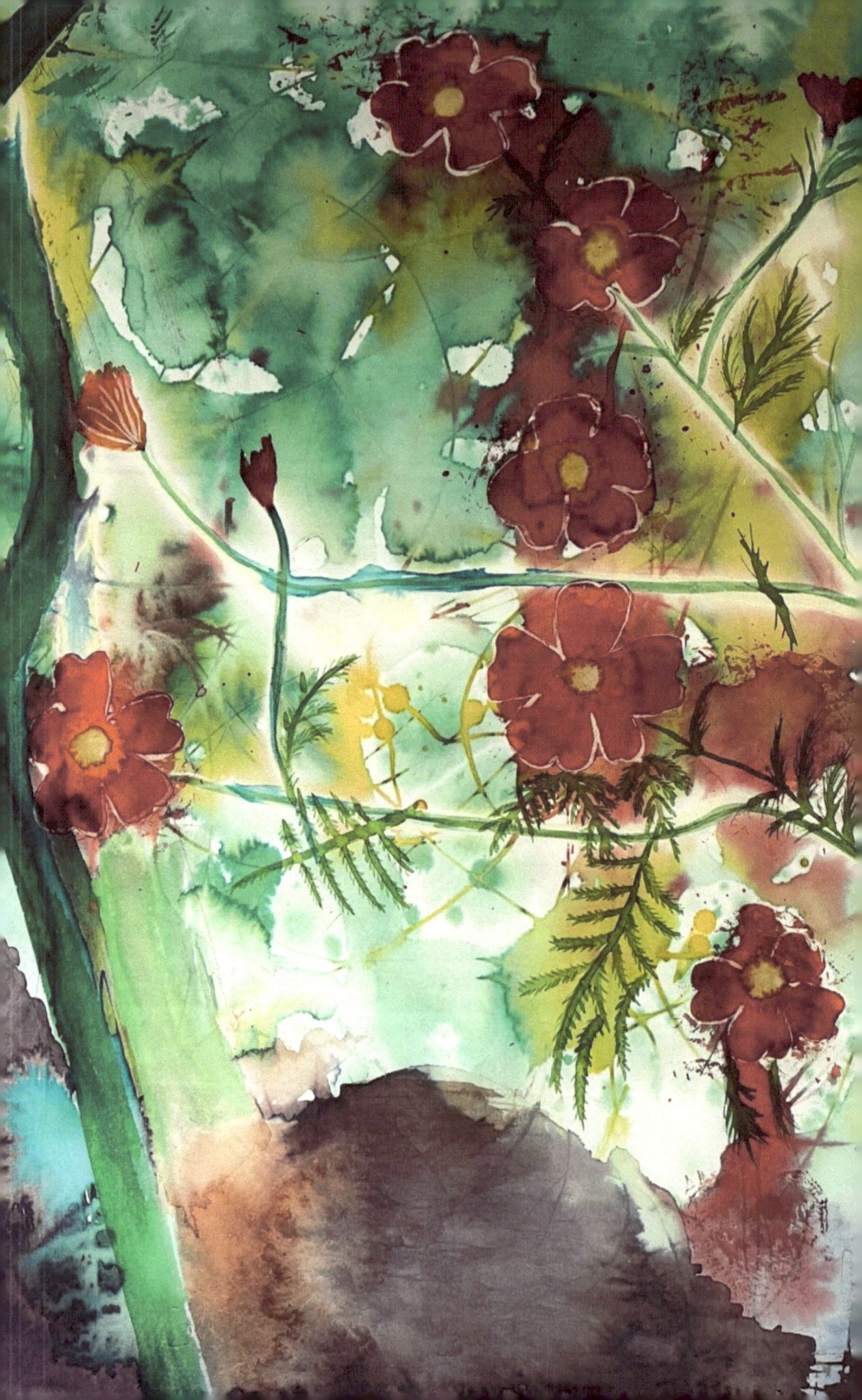

www.ingramcontent.com/pod-product-compliance
Lightning Source LLC
Chambersburg PA
CBHW050752290526
45792CB00008B/2150